STOCKHOLM - SWEDEN
At Your Fingertips

by

Alison Allfrey
&
Jessica Dölling Gripberg

This book is dedicated to all those who adventure in Sweden in the hope that they will learn to love and be inspired by it as much as we are.

With so many thanks to our families, who have been patient while we have worked on this book and to the fantastic working relationship we have forged together during the difficult months of Covid and numerous lockdowns in 2020 and 2021.

We began writing this book as countries were being affected by the Covid-19 pandemic. Thanks to modern technology, we have been able to work from our homes in the UK and Sweden and discuss the book constantly using videoconferencing – who would have thought this sort of project would be possible remotely? We can't wait to meet up again in Stockholm.

Table of Contents

Introduction to Sweden   1

The Quickest of Histories   2

Sweden Today   4

Getting to the Heart of the Matter   7
Swedish Maxims   7
Proverbs   8

The Swedish Language   9

First Impressions   10

Starting Out   12

International Schools   16
BISS – The British International School of Stockholm   16
SIS – Swedish International School   16
The German School in Stockholm   16
The French International School in Stockholm - Lycée Francais Saint Louis   16
Förskola (previously called *Dagis*)   17
Nurseries/Pre-schools   17
Pre-Schools   17

Getting Your Bearings   18
Roads   18
Airports   18
Trains   19
Ferries   19

Meeting People   21
Clubs   21
The International Women's Club of Stockholm   21
American Club of Sweden   21
American Women's Club   21
Meet Up   21
Rotary Club International of Stockholm   22
Internations   22
Stockholm Accueil   22
Chambers of Commerce   22
Stockholm Chamber of Commerce   22
American Chamber of Commerce in Sweden   22
British Chamber of Commerce   22
French Chamber of Commerce   22
German / Swedish Chamber of Commerce   22
The Dutch Chamber in Sweden   22
Italian Chamber of Commerce   22

Places to Stay   23
Short Term Accommodation   23
Accomodation and Workspace   23
Hotels   23

Soulful Places   25
St James's Church - *St Jakob*   25
The Stockholm Cathedral - *Storkyrkan*   25
St Gertrude - *Tyska Kyrkan*   26
Djursholms Kapell   26
Hedvig Eleonora   26
Anglican Church - *Engelska Kyrkan*   26
Catholic Churches   27
Synagogues   27
Mosques   27

Shopping   28
Seasonal Essentials   28

Your Personal Number & Benefits   30
Personnummer   30
Swedish Social Insurance   30

Pets   32

Food   33

The Swedish *Julbord*   40

Drink & Alcohol   42

Food Shopping   44

Going to the Supermarket   46
Flour   46
Types of sugar   47
Bread, biscuits and crispbreads   47
Miscellaneous   47
Butter (*Smör*) & Margarine (*Margarin*)   48
Cheese (*Ost*)   48
Milk (*Mjölk*)   49
Sour Cream   50
Yoghurt (yogurt)   50
Other yoghurts   50
Fish & Seafood   50
Fruits   51
Vegetables   52
Meat   53

Restaurants   55
Sturehof   56
Prinsen   56

Grodan   56
KB (*Konstnärsbaren*)   57
Berns   57
Ulla Winbladh   57
Ulriksdals Värdshus   57
Stallmästaregården   57
Pelikan   57
Gondolen   58
Kvarnen   58
Eating in Djursholm   58
Eating on Lidingö   59

The Best *Fika*   60
Grillska Huset – Stortorget, Gamla Stan   61
Chokladkoppen – Stortorget, Gamla Stan   61
Tössebageriet - Karlavägen 77   61
Petite France - John Ericssonsgatan 6   61
Vetekatten - Kungsgatan 55   61

***Godis*   62**

Stockholm Nightlife   63
Bars   63
Pubs   64
Night Clubs   64

Health   65
Going to the doctor   65
Hair, Skin & Medical Conditions   65

Driving & Parking   69

Clothes Shopping   74
Shopping in Stockholm   74
Shopping centres outside Stockholm   75
Shopping for the seasons – don't get caught out!   76
Online shopping   77

Sports Shopping   78
Incredible choice for all seasons   78
Second-hand sports equipment   79

Books   80
Reading Suggestions   80
The Saga of Gosta Berling - *Gösta Berling's Saga*   80
Doctor Glas - *Doktor Glas*   80
City of my Dreams - *Mina Drömmars Stad*   81
The Emigrants - *Utvandrarna*   81
The Expedition - The Forgotten Story of a Polar Tragedy   81
Astrid and Veronika   81
So Sweden – Living Differently   82

The Almost Nearly Perfect People –   82
Swedish Crime   **82**
The Girl with the Dragon Tattoo   83
The Ice Princess, The Preacher, The Stonecutter   83
Swedish Classics   **83**

Swedish books for children   84

Astrid Lindgren   84
Elsa Beskow   84
Sven Nordqvist   85
Tove Jansson   85

Films and series   86

The Cold Swedish Winter   86
Welcome to Sweden   86
A Man Called Ove   86
The Hundred Year Old Man who Climbed out of the Window and Disappeared 87
The Girl with the Dragon Tattoo   87
Bron   87

Painters & Sculptors   88

Carl Larsson (1853-1919)   88
Anders Zorn (1860-1920)   88
Bruno Liljefors (1860-1939)   89
Carl Wilhelmson (1866-1928)   89
Carl Eldh (1873-1954)   89
Carl Milles (1875 – 1955)   90
John Bauer (1882-1918)   90

Art Galleries   91

The National Museum   91
Fotografiska   91
Artipelag   91
Waldemarsudde   92
Liljevalchs   92
Thielska Galleriet   93
Millesgården   93

Swedish Design   94

Working in Sweden   96

Getting Outside   99

Running and walking   99
Cycling   101
Tennis   102
Golf   102
Gyms   103
Yoga   103
Pilates   104
Padel   104

Indoor Swimming Pools   104
Riding   105
Summer Swimming   105
Winter Swimming   106
Bastu - Sauna   107

Getting Around on the Water   **108**
Ferries   108
Private Boat/Rentals   110
Fishing   113

Winter Sports   **114**
Skating   114
Skiing   116
Cross-country skiing   117

What is *Vasaloppet*?   **121**

Other Outdoor Activities   **122**
Dog sledding   122
Snöskoter – Snowmobiling   122
Ice Driving   122

Gardens, Flora and Fauna   **123**
Gardens and islands to visit   123
Swedish flowers   124
Swedish trees   125
Animals – the rare and wonderful   125

Learning Swedish   **127**
Language, finding your feet and reading between the lines   127
Lidgard Education   127
Swedish for Professionals   128
New in Sweden   128
Tree Coaching   128

A Quick Swedish Lesson   **129**
Greetings   130
In a café   131
In a shop   131
At the doctor's   131

Social Life & Customs   **133**
At a Swedish home   133
Dinner etiquette   135
How to toast   136

Keeping Up To Date   **137**
The Local   137
Mundus International   137
SR & SVT   137

Soaking Up The Seasons   **139**
Winter   139
Spring   139
Summer   140
Autumn   140

The Swedish Year   **141**
January   **141**
Vikingarännet   141
Ice Skating in and around Stockholm   141
Skiing near Stockholm   142
February/March   **142**
Fettisdagen - Shrove Tuesday   142
March   **142**
25th March *Våffeldagen* or *Vårfrudagen* – Waffle Day   142
Easter – *Påsk*   143
April   **143**
1st April - April Fools' Day!   143
30th April *Valborgsmässoafton* - Walpurgis   143
30th April The Birthday of H. M. King Carl XVI Gustaf   144
May   **144**
1st May – May Day   144
Mothers' Day   144
Gärdesloppet - Prince Bertil Memorial   144
June   **144**
Studenten - Graduation   144
6th June - Swedish National Day   144
Midsummer Eve   145
July   **145**
Summer holidays!   145
August   **145**
Crayfish time   145
Surströmming time   146
September   **146**
Running challenges   146
Autumn fair   146
Mushroom picking time   146
October   **147**
4th October *Kanelbullens Dag* – Cinnamon Bun Day   147
Halloween (not traditionally a Swedish custom)   147
November   **147**
Allhelgonsdagen - All Saints Day   147
Fathers' Day   147
(2nd Sunday in November)   147
11th November *Mårten Gås* - St Martin's Day   147
December   **148**
1st December - Winter Tyres   148

Advent   148
Christmas Markets   148
10th December – The Nobel Day   148
13th December - *Lucia*   149
24th December – *Julafton*   149
25th December – *Juldagen*   150

For Children   **151**
Junibacken   151
Post Museum   151
Tekniska Museet   152
Police Museum   152
Maritime Museum   152
The *Vasa*   153
The Royal Stables & Changing of the Guard   153
ArkDes - the museum of architecture and design   154
Stockholm Toy Museum   154
Gamla Stans Polkagriskokeri   154
Christmas tree, lights, displays, markets   154
The ABBA Museum   155
Gröna Lund   156
The Viking Museum   156
Armémuseum   156
Skansen   157
Naturhistoriska Riksmuseet   157
The Butterfly House & Ocean Aquarium   157
Sweden International Horse Show   158
Events at Avicii Arena (previously known as *Globen*)   158
Best parks and rides in Stockholm   159
Soft play - Indoor playgrounds *Lekland*   159
Kulturhuset   159
Space   160
Ocean bus   160

Outside Stockholm   **161**
Tom Tits Experiment   161
Kolmården   161
Järvzoo   161

Sports Activities for Children   **163**
Sailing   163
Ice Skating/Ice Hockey   163
Gymnastics   164
Sports Camps etc.   164
Other activities for children   164

How to get around in Stockholm   **165**
Taxi   165
Public Transport   165

By Boat   166

Castles Near Stockholm   **169**

Skokloster   169
Taxinge Slott   169
Gripsholm   170
Steninge Slott   171
Näsby Slott   171
Ulfsunda Slott   171
Hesselby Slott   171
Görvälns Slott   172
Rosersbergs Slott   172
The Royal Palace, Stockholm   172
Drottningholm (UNESCO world heritage site)   173
Royal Swedish Palaces   175

More Palaces & Castles   **176**

Museums   **178**

Post Museum   178
Army Museum   178
Museum of Ethnography   178
Museum of Mediterranean & Near Eastern Antiquities   178
Museum of Far Eastern Antiquities   178
The Hallwyl Collection   179
The Swedish History Museum - *Historiska*   179
The Royal Armoury - *Livrustkammaren*   179
Maritime Museum   180
The *Vasa*   180
The Royal Stables and Changing of the Guard   181
The Modern Museum   182
Nationalmuseum   182
The Medieval Museum - *Medeltidsmuseet*   183
The ABBA Museum   183
Gröna Lund - colloquially called *Grönan*   183
The Viking Museum   184
Skansen   184
Naturhistoriska Riksmuseet   185
The Nobel Prize Museum   185
The Nordic Museum   185
The City Hall   186
Riddarholmskyrkan   186
The House of Nobility – *Riddarhuset*   187

Music, Concerts & Theatre   **188**

Operahuset (the Opera House)   188
Berwaldhallen   189
Konserthuset   189
The Royal Dramatic Theatre - *Dramaten*   189

Drottningholmsteatern   189
Stockholm English Speaking Theatre   190
International Theatre Stockholm   190

Swedish Music   191

Day trips from Stockholm   194
Sigtuna   194
Uppsala   195
Trosa   196
Mariefred   196

Overnight Trips & Hikes   197
Lake Vättern (1 or 2 nights – summertime)   197
West Coast of Sweden (summertime)   198
Sörmlandsleden trail (1,000 kilometres long)   200
Dalarna (3 days - summertime)   201
Dalarna (wintertime)   203
The Jämtland Triangle (3 day hike - summertime)   204
Kungsleden & Kebnekaise (summertime)   205

Unusual Places To Stay   206
Grinda, Finnhamn & Sandhamn   206
Fejan or Island Lodge   207
Tree Hotel   207
Utter Inn or Jumbo Jet   207
Ice Hotel   207
Igloo   208
Arctic Gourmet Cabin or Nyrup   208

Public Holidays   209

A Selection of Swedish Recipes   210
Conversion tables   210
Self-raising flour   211
Köttbullar – Swedish Meatballs   212
Gravad Lax – Cured Salmon   213
Gravlaxsås   213
Waffle Batter   214
Kanelbullar - Cinnamon Buns   215
Semlor   217

Recycling in Sweden   219
Recycling points/stations - *Sopstation/Återvinningsstation*   219
Food/Organic waste   220
Recycling Centres - *Återvinningscentral*   221
Bulky waste   221
Hazardous waste   221
Normal Household/Residual waste (non-recyclable)   222
What can we pour down the drain?   222
Pant   222

Medicines   222

Guided Tours   **223**

Useful Contacts & Websites   **224**
Grow Internationals   224
New in Sweden (New in Danderyd)   224
Newbie Guide   224
Undutchables   224
Thats up   224
Your Living City   225
Visit Sweden   225
Visit Stockholm   225
ToStockholm   225

Emergency & Helplines   **226**
Government Information   226
Hesa Fredrik – Hoarse Fredrik   226
'If Crisis or War Comes' Brochure   226
Crisis Information   227
112 - SOS   227
113 13 – Information number (in case of accidents and crises)   227
114 14 – Police (not urgent)   227
1177 – Medical Advice (not urgent)   227
116 111 - Child Helpline   227
116 123 - Emotional Support Helpline   227
90101 Suicide Prevention - *Självmordslinjen*   227
Sweden's National Women's Helpline - *Kvinnofridslinjen*   228
The National Association of Swedish Crisis Centres for Men   228

Disclaimer   **230**

Personal Notes   **231**

STOCKHOLM - SWEDEN
At Your Fingertips

Introduction to Sweden

Welcome to Sweden! *Välkommen*! This is a phrase you will hear time without number now you've arrived in Sweden. The other will be, 'How do you like Sweden?'. Why? Because the Swedes are hugely proud of their vast, pristine, beautiful country and think, quite fairly, that it's the most wonderful country in the world. How refreshing!

Sweden is a country of paradoxes – at the cutting edge of innovation and very liberal in its thinking, but at the same time hugely traditional and a country which ticks to the beat of nature's clock and the festivals of ancient lore. Determined that people should be accountable for themselves, self-sufficient and pragmatic, whilst also having an all-pervasive state system with an astonishing amount of personal data at its fingertips. Intensely focused on the outdoors and all its pleasures across the seasons, but with the younger generation often shunning this in favour of the temptations of technology. Above all, Sweden is unique and stands on its own, not just with its very northerly geographic position, but also because its pulse is simply different and takes quite some understanding. But it's a challenge worth taking on, because the rewards are fantastic and so worthwhile. Perhaps Sweden is a country which is very easy to admire, but much harder to live in – at first.

This book is written by people who have lived abroad, who have lived in Sweden, who understand the particular needs of expats, foreigners or newcomers and who love what Sweden has to offer as well as being realistic about its idiosyncrasies. We very much hope that *'Stockholm - Sweden at Your Fingertips'* will prove a faithful friend to tuck into your bag as you discover Sweden's delights and a reliable companion to help you as you forge your relationship with this unique country.

The Quickest of Histories

Sweden has been an imperial power, a land of mass exodus and many things in between. The evolution of Sweden, Norway and Denmark from Viking maritime supremacies to Christian countries in shades of bubbling rivalry and tenuous unity in the eleventh century perhaps explains the continued dynamics of Scandinavia today. The transition allowed Scandinavia to begin to be influenced by western European culture and the rise of the Hanseatic League between the 13th and 15th centuries sealed these countries' fate as hugely powerful Baltic traders.

By 1523, Sweden had flexed its muscles under the newly established monarchy of Gustav Vasa enough to wriggle away from subservient union with Denmark under King Kristian II of Denmark and the horrific Stockholm Bloodbath, paving the way for more than a hundred years of wealth and influence. This was then consolidated upon, with Sweden regaining southern states previously under Danish control as part of the proliferation of wars and disputes which characterised Swedish / Danish relations for much of the 17th century, culminating in Sweden's triumphant invasion of Jutland across frozen seas in 1657 and the acquiescence of Denmark in the Treaty of Roskilde in Denmark in 1660. Sweden's imperial might was at its apogée, though it was assailed by a belligerent union of Russia, Poland and Denmark again in 1700 which would see its power and spoils decimated.

Sweden would then forge a union with Norway in 1814 – which endured until 1905 – each with its own laws but under the same monarch, as a result of the treaty of Kiel. Karl XIII (a.k.a. Karl II of Norway) was childless and an heir had to be found. First, Prince Christian August of Denmark became heir-presumptive to the throne before dying later that same year by falling off his horse from an apparent stroke. The country then turned to a Marshal in Napoleon's army, General Jean-Baptiste Bernadotte, who moved to Sweden with his reluctant wife and son and was adopted by the ailing King. When the old King died in 1818, Jean Baptiste Bernadotte became King Karl

XIV Johan of Sweden. The current Swedish King Carl XVI Gustav is the seventh monarch after Jean Baptist Bernadotte and still part of the Bernadotte Dynasty. His heir apparent is his daughter Victoria, Crown Princess of Sweden.

Sweden's first Social Democrat government was elected in 1920, setting out to create a thoroughly liberal state and stable social welfare system, whilst paving the way for neutrality which Sweden maintained through the First World War. The equilibrium of Scandinavian peace was toppled once more during the Second World War. Norway and Denmark were occupied by the Germans whilst Sweden juggled with its neutrality - granting the transit of German troops through the country whilst assisting the Allies with information derived from encrypted messages the Germans sent utilising Swedish telephone wires. Within two weeks the code to these encrypted German messages had been cracked by Swedish cryptographer Arne Beurling and information would 'leak' to the Allies. During the war Stockholm was sometimes referred to as the 'Casablanca of the North', with a flow of refugees, businessmen and diplomats, not to mention spies and secret agents exchanging classified information.

Sweden Today

Sweden joined the UN in 1946 and showed its prescient egalitarian thinking by granting the Order of Succession in 1979, whereby both male and female heirs could succeed to the throne. The then Crown Prince Carl Philip lost his title to his elder sister Victoria who is now Crown Princess.

Sweden suffered profound shock when its Socialist Prime Minister, Olof Palme, was shot in 1986, but building up its core industries of steel, ball bearings, paper pulp and matches since the mid nineteenth century and becoming a member of the EU in 1995, it has been transformed from a country in abject poverty following the First World War, to a place of wealth, peace and with a welfare state – *Folkhemmet* – which is the envy of the world. Today, Sweden remains at the forefront of progressive, environmentally friendly thinking, be that through the astonishing rise of teenage protagonist Greta Thunberg who has challenged the UN, the climate debate and her elders with total fearlessness, or through Sweden's singular and fascinatingly individual take on how to approach Covid 19 under the guidance of epidemiologist, Anders Tegnell.

All public power proceeds from the people. This is the foundation of the Swedish governmental system. Everyone has equal rights and free access to scrutinise how politicians and public agencies exercise their power.

Swedes are phenomenal with statistics and records and if you think you might originate from Sweden and want to check your ancestry, the Swedish National Archives date back 400 years and are amongst the oldest in the world. The country also has very comprehensive and easily available information about salaries and taxes, so there is much greater transparency about these than you might be used to.

Of the more than 10 million Swedes living in Sweden, the majority live in the 3 largest cities - Stockholm, Göteborg and Malmö and, at 1.9 births per woman, the country's fertility rate ranks amongst the highest in Europe probably due to the generous 480 days paid parental leave. Today, about one-fifth of Sweden's population has an immigrant background.

The Sami who live in the northern part of Scandinavia are part of Sweden's indigenous population. They are estimated at around 80,000 people, spread over four countries with approximately 20,000 in Sweden, 50,000 in Norway, 8,000 in Finland and 2,000 in Russia.

Sweden is a parliamentary democracy, which means that all public power proceeds from the people. General elections are held every four years to vote for a political party that will be represented in the Swedish parliament, the *Riksdag*. This is made up of 349 political representatives from eight different parties of which, at the time of writing, the three largest are the Social Democrats, New Moderates and Sweden Democrats. The next elections will be held in 2022.

During the elections they also vote for the regional/county councils (*region*) and municipalities (*kommun*). Non-Swedish citizens from other countries are eligible to vote in these but have to be registered as resident in Sweden for more than three consecutive years before election day.

5

There are Four fundamental laws that make up the Swedish Constitution:

The Instrument of Government
This Guarantees citizens the right to obtain information freely, hold demonstrations, form political parties and practice their religion.

The Act of Succession
This regulates the right of members of the House of Bernadotte, the Swedish royal family, to accede to the Swedish throne. This was last modified in 1980 to allow the first born, whether female or male, to become heir to the throne.

The Freedom of the Press Act
This gives the public free access to official documents relating to the work of the parliament, the government and public agencies. This law allows people to study all official documents whenever they wish. It is therefore easy to find out how much people earn in Sweden from official tax declarations.

The Fundamental Law on Freedom of Expression
This came into force in 1992 and largely mirrors the Freedom of the Press Act, as regards the prohibition of censorship, the freedom to communicate information and the right to anonymity.

The latest important law to be adopted in Sweden and which came into effect in 2020, is the UN's Convention of the Right of the Child. This treaty is based on a profound idea: that children are not just objects who belong to their parents and for whom decisions are made, or adults in training. Rather, they are human beings and individuals with their own rights. It is worth being aware of this, as smacking your child is not tolerated in Sweden and may have serious repercussions.

Getting to the Heart of the Matter

Swedish Maxims
Sweden is encapsulated and propelled by a number of strong maxims, centred mostly around the concepts of self-sufficiency, a no-nonsense attitude and humility. These will be explained later on, but in Sweden you have the definite feeling that there is a code of behaviour and it helps to try to understand this.

In particular, people like to be self-contained so it is worth remembering not to invade their space and to expect no, or just a cursory greeting (*hej!*) if you see someone when walking.

Here are a few which reflect the Swedish way of doing things:

Allemansrätten
The freedom to roam, or 'everyman's right', epitomises the Swedish Socialist ideal and refers to the public's right to access certain public or privately owned land, lakes, and rivers for recreation and exercise. The right is sometimes called the right of public access to the wilderness or the 'right to roam'.

Fika

Fika is a veritable institution in Sweden and the best way to catch your breath, socialise with friends or colleagues and get the lowdown.

Literally meaning coffee break, it is actually a welcome excuse for large amounts of strong, restorative coffee and even more restorative cakes, ideally a cardamom or cinnamon bun. These will slow the bloodflow but boost morale immeasurably.

Flygskam

First entering common parlance in early 2020, it literally translates as 'flight shame'. It is a climate change movement, which encourages people to stop travelling by plane.

Lagom

Swedes adhere strongly to a keen instinct for doing and saying what is just enough, not too much, not showy, not indulgent. It's a maxim of modesty, pragmatism and keeping your feet firmly on the ground. It doesn't do to have grand ideas about yourself or, indeed, try to be very different from anyone else. For example, the formidable Ingvar Kamprad, founder and sole owner of IKEA, always made a point of flying economy and staying in budget hotels on business trips.

Proverbs

'*Borta bra, men hemma bäst*'
'There's no place like home'

'*Bra karl reder sig själv*'
'Every man for himself'

'*Eget beröm luktar illa*'
'Don't blow your own trumpet' (meaning don't boast)

Ingen ko på isen
Literally – 'There's no cow on the ice' or more idiomatically 'it's just water under the bridge'.

The Swedish Language

The Swedish language is a North Germanic language developed from Old Norse, as is Norwegian and Danish. This makes it easy for the Scandinavians to interact in 'Scandinavian', although at times Swedes tend to find the more guttural Danish impossible to decipher and will switch to English.

Finnish is a totally different proposition originating from a Finno-Ugric language (as do Hungarian, Estonian and Sami) but with their historical connection to Sweden, 5% of the Finns still speak Swedish as their native language. Finland includes Swedish in its school curriculum. Incidentally, there are also five official national minority languages in Sweden – Finnish, all Sami dialects, Torne Valley Finnish (Meänkieli), Romani, and Yiddish. This is to ensure that the languages used by public bodies are 'protected, simple, and comprehensible'.

First Impressions

The first impressions you may have of Sweden are of enormous space, emptiness, room to breathe, clean air. On the positive side, these may make you feel liberated, inspired to relish the great outdoors, keen to try new things. On the flip side, you may feel isolated, confused, all at sea. This mix of emotions is entirely normal, and you may grapple with them whilst also wondering how you can afford to live in what seems like an extremely expensive country. It is true that eating out in restaurants, especially if you would like to drink alcohol too, can take its toll on your pocket, but lunchtime can be more reasonable and after a period of adjustment and working out what to choose in the supermarket, you can eat without going bankrupt.

The other very noticeable thing about Sweden is quite how seasonal it is. Not only are the seasons extreme, with a possible variation of up to 50 degrees Celsius (122 Fahrenheit) between the height of summer and the depths of winter, but this has an enormous effect on what people do and what is open. So you need to focus your mind on how to get the most out of the long summer and winter seasons, savour the short sweetness of spring and manage the slight gloom of autumn (notwithstanding its glorious colours). The key is to have the right clothing, watch how Swedes are spending their time and visit as many of Sweden's wonderful castles and summer delights as you can in the summer – blink and you'll miss them!

It is comparatively warm in Stockholm given Sweden's extreme northern location. Stockholm's latitude position (59.334591) compares with that of Anchorage in Alaska and St. Petersburg in Russia. Thanks to the Gulf Stream which carries warm water across the Atlantic, survival in Stockholm is possible! Because of this latitude it is very dark in winter and very light in summer.

You will notice once you arrive in Sweden that cash is used very infrequently. Some shops do not even accept cash as payment! A frequent payment method primarily used for small amounts is called *Swish* - it is an app downloaded on your mobile and available once you have a Swedish bank account.

Starting Out

It's important to remember that moving a person, a couple or indeed a whole family to an entirely new country, where everything is unknown and challenging, is a huge adventure but can also be daunting, exhausting and stressful. Often the stresses can land on the person who is trying to hold the family together, so if this is you, don't expect too much of yourself and be prepared for a feeling of initial fear, followed by possible elation during the honeymoon period of finding everything new and exciting – and then perhaps a bit of a slump as you realise this new, slightly bewildering life is here to stay.

It takes a lot of patience and courage to find your feet, and the people and places which make you feel secure. And the same goes for children who have been uprooted, who will probably hanker after certain things from home and may take some time to settle. In the meantime, they may blame you for everything that goes wrong!

Fortunately ex-pat schools are full of children in the same boat, many of whom have been through the experience before and hence there is an incredibly welcoming, embracing atmosphere which fosters friendships and breaking down the barriers quickly. This can be contrary to the nursery experience – as so many children go part- or full-time from a very early age, you may find yourself missing the play groups, singing and sausages for kids' tea which you may have had at home, but of course there are opportunities to make friends from a young age too. And if you can't find things happening which you would like, you can always invent them! Living as an expat is incredibly liberating in that way.

Here is an extract from *So Sweden – Living Differently*, by Alison Allfrey which reflects some of the issues encountered by an expat family:

Tom, meanwhile, was curiously subdued, stoic at school, but somehow, having been wrenched away from his beloved home, he was without his habitual twinkle. An element of this was probably that we had been forced to leave the base of his bed in his tiny bedroom, as it simply wouldn't fit out of the door, so he had valiantly survived on a mere mattress to date. Installed in his new Swedish bed after an afternoon surrounded by Swedish design shopping opportunities, with its trademark hard base and thin mattress but rather wonderful imposing headboard, he looked more at one with himself. But something was missing. He had had such hopes of meeting Swedish children on the huge communal grassy play area behind our house, replete with seesaw and swings, but we had soon realised that full time parental work precluded play of that sort and the swings remained defiantly empty. He had envisaged chatting in Swedish, but had realised that a mere 40 minutes of lessons per week might not suffice. So, age immaterial, meeting our neighbours' daughter Hanna was momentous.

Ed, of course, had maintained that any quietness from Tom was either in my imagination or of my own creation to some unclear end. Testimony to the fully English blood coursing through his veins, counter to the Welsh flowing in mine, Ed had decided ab initio that all would be well, nobody must flinch and none of us would notice at all that we were in a different country, not in our own home and without our family and friends. Anything else would be ridiculous, an indulgence, an allowance for faltering from Tom and hence not to be entertained. Stiff upper lip indeed. And what that suppresses!

I had found from my previous experience of spending a year in France, that those left behind in England had whinnied with excitement at the prospect of the chance to live abroad, knowing full well that they had never moved beyond England themselves and hence exerting unseen pressure on me to make it a success. The same was true in Sweden. My mother had said I was lucky and shouldn't complain. All well and good, but there was no denying that this wholesale changing of all the foundations of our life was not without reverberations. Mixed emotions. Wonder at the swift kindness and openness of ex-pats, seemingly without the need to hang in the wings for ten years while you were assessed from every angle which can plague a move to a new area in England. Wonder too at the utter emptiness of every single house surrounding ours, from dawn until dusk every day of the working week. Thank heavens for Tara around the corner, safely at hand in Lökevägen and her silky flat coat retriever, Saffie, needing walks with comforting regularity and hence facilitating much needed chat.'

Having children or a pet obviously helps ease your way into a social environment but otherwise joining as many clubs, activities and associations as possible is hugely rewarding. You just need to meet one friend to have as a sounding board and ally to help you in your first transitional months in Sweden – and it is far more fun exploring your new surroundings together.

Depending on when you arrive in Sweden, your priorities will differ. Firstly, of course, you will need somewhere to live and may be lucky enough to have a relocation agency already in place before moving to Sweden. If not, here are some of the main ones:

Humanentrance.com
Alfamoving.com

Expatarrivals.com
Keyrelocation.se
Nimmersion.com
Nrgab.com (Nordic Relocation)
Primerelocation.com

Finding accommodation is a number one priority and many choose to live close to the international schools if they have children.

Listed below are some of the areas outside Stockholm, but within easy touching distance, which are most popular amongst expats and diplomats with families: Sollentuna, Täby; NäsbyPark, Danderyd, Djursholm, Solna, Lidingö and Bromma.

International Schools

There are a growing number of international schools in and around Stockholm, but here are some of the best established:

BISS – The British International School of Stockholm
Based in the lovely surroundings of Djursholm, just 15 minutes outside Stockholm, the school caters for children from the age of 3 to 16 on two sites. It offers an excellent education following an international curriculum. It is particularly welcoming to expats and has a very active PPA. Note that it isn't particularly British, but rather incredibly cosmopolitan, with families from 50 different nationalities.
www.bisstockholm.se

SIS – Swedish International School
An excellent international school based in Östermalm and best suited for families living in Stockholm itself. It is a very large, dynamic and multi-cultural school which works towards the International Baccalaureat.
www.stockholmis.se

The German School in Stockholm
With a 400 year track record, the school offers a curriculum taught in both German and Swedish, working towards the German International High School Diploma and Swedish diploma.
www.tyskaskolan.se

The French International School in Stockholm - Lyçée Francais Saint Louis
Children aged 6 to 18 are taught the French curriculum, whilst there is a pre-school which teaches according to the Swedish system. Results are excellent and children in the French system work towards the Brevet and Baccalaureat. Based in Östermalm.
www.lfsl.net

Förskola (previously called *Dagis*)
From the age of about two most Swedish children attend *förskola*.
Some also go to a *dagmamma* who usually takes care of a smaller
group of children. Before that you can attend an *öppen förskola* (play
group) with your child - a great way of meeting other parents. Check
with your local municipality where these are - many of them are run
by the local church.

Nurseries/Pre-schools
Futuraskolan is probably the best known chain of international,
English-speaking day nurseries. In Djursholm, there is a very
charming, small nursery called Lilla Montessori.

Pre-Schools
Engelska Förskolan & Engelsk Franska Förskolan
www.engelskaforskolan.se

Getting Your Bearings

Roads
Apart from being in a stunning position at the edge of Lake Mälaren to the west and the Baltic Sea and its wonderful archipelago to the east, Stockholm lies at the crossroads of two key motorways. The E18 goes west, past the top of one of Sweden's two greatest lakes, Lake Vänern and on all the way to Oslo – about a six hour trip. To the north-east, it takes you to Norrtälje and on to the coast. The E4 runs north-south – up past Uppsala, Sundsvall and then to the very northern reaches of the country and south / south-west past Jönköping (beware of speed traps and turn west if you want to go to Gothenburg) and down all the way to Copenhagen, via Lund, Sweden's diminutive but charming university city and across the magnificent Öresund bridge.

Airports
Arlanda is the main airport for international flights and is 40 minutes north of Stockholm up the E4. There is an airport train – the Arlanda Express - which leaves from T-Centralen in Stockholm and gets you there in less than 20 minutes, as well as lots of airport buses. You will find good short- or longer-term parking very close to the airport. This is probably the most serene airport you will ever travel through, replete with signature Swedish wooden panelling throughout and a Swedish hall of fame as you come into arrivals (think Björn Borg, Ingemar Bergman, ABBA...).

The two other main, much smaller airports are Västerås, about 100km west of Stockholm which has Ryanair flights to Spain and the UK, and Skavsta about 100km south-west of Stockholm, with flights across Europe with Ryanair and Wizz Air. Whether these will survive the repercussions of the pandemic remains to be seen.

Bromma Airport is the European Domestic Airport with connections to the north and south of Sweden. Whereas other European airports can be paralysed by snow, Swedish airports take it all in their stride and continue as normal, in all but the very worst weather.

Trains
The Central Station in Stockholm, the City Terminal (local commuter trains) and Arlanda Express (airport shuttle) are all centrally located under the same roof at T-Centralen. Travelling by train to other parts of Sweden is a comfortable way of seeing the country - there is also the high-speed railway, X2000, which takes you from Stockholm to Gothenburg (3hrs), Malmö (4 ½ hrs) or Copenhagen (5hrs). You can comfortably access the underground/subway (Tunnelbana) from T-Centralen without having to go outside.

Ferries
You can reach Sweden by ferry from mainland Europe, though this is more difficult than it used to be. The best route is probably from / to Gothenburg from Kiel in northern Germany, which takes 14 hours with Stena Line.

The Stockholm archipelago has fantastic ferry services running to many of the islands. These are detailed in the Boating section.

Otherwise, you will see beguiling blue signs with promises of St. Petersburg, Tallinn and Helsinki as you drive through Stockholm. This is because there are ferries to these cities from the Värtahamnen and Stadsgården ports in the city. Cruises are available from a number of companies including Viking Line, Silja Line, Direct Ferries and Nordic Cruises. Beware that these can be quite raucous and alcohol fuelled, as prices are cheaper than in Sweden and the buffet restaurants can be something of a bun fight. But there are fabulous trips available, where you can take in three capitals in three days or longer. It's best to go in the summer, when you can have cocktails on the top deck and then dinner watching the never-ending sun.

For the really determined, ferries go throughout the winter, perhaps with an icebreaker on the front (the noise of which may hamper a good night's sleep). This is a fantastic way to get a taste of Russia, Finland and Estonia and children love the novelty of sleeping on the ferry and waking up to a new country each morning. It's worth getting a guide for the St Petersburg leg if possible as there's so much to take in within a very short space of time. As Russian visas can be notoriously difficult to get from Sweden, this is the perfect way of getting a glimpse of St. Petersburg without all the paperwork as no visa is necessary.

Other ferries go from Nynäshamn to Gotland on the east coast, famed for its wonderful beaches and Visby, the stunning Hanseatic town with its yellow and orange hues. Or you might like to venture to Åland to the north-east of Stockholm from Kapellskär or Grisslehamn. This island is a fascinating mix of Swedish language and Finnish culture, not to mention the vestiges of Russian military imperialism - a beautiful place for its space, amazing apple juice, remote beaches and coastline with large rocks shelving into the sea. There are apocryphal stories that this is a particularly difficult place to navigate when sailing, as the Finns have never produced maps of its waters for fear of a return of the Russians.

www.directferries.co.uk
www.nordic.cruises
www.destinationgotland.se
www.tallinksilja.se
www.siljaline.se
www.vikingline.se

Meeting People

As we have mentioned, it may seem a bit tricky getting to know Swedes and feeling that you belong. Initially you will probably have plenty to do but after the 'honeymoon' period, a spot of loneliness may set in unless you have children in international schools, which often have a good parent association. The best way is to dive right in and join as many clubs as possible - you just might find that one person who will make all the difference to your stay in Sweden. There are plenty of clubs as well as Chambers of Commerce for networking - we have listed a few below.

Clubs

The International Women's Club of Stockholm
Bringing together women of all ages and nationalities: those living in Stockholm for a short or long period of time, for private reasons or for work and looking to get in touch with other international ladies. The IWC Stockholm may just be the right forum for you to meet new friends.
www.iwcstockholm.se

American Club of Sweden
The American Club functions in the spirit of its founding members - providing good fellowship and being of assistance to both residents of and newcomers to the country.
www.americanclub.se

American Women's Club
Provides a sense of fellowship to American women living abroad.
www.awcstockholm.org

Meet Up
Meetup is a service used to organise online groups that host in-person and virtual events for people with similar interests.
www.meetup.com

Rotary Club International of Stockholm
The only Rotary club in Stockholm that conducts meetings in English. The membership is international, culturally diverse and has representatives from several embassies as well as from the business, professional, vocational and artistic sectors.
www.stockholm-international@rotary.se

Internations
They arrange an array of events in Stockholm as well as in other parts of the world. A community for expats and also when travelling on business around the world - Internations is there to make you feel at home wherever you are.
www.internations.org

Stockholm Accueil
For Francophones - they arrange a variety of events and activities.
www.stockholmaccueil.se

Chambers of Commerce

Stockholm Chamber of Commerce
www.english.chamber.se
American Chamber of Commerce in Sweden
www.amcham.se
British Chamber of Commerce
www.bscc.info
French Chamber of Commerce
www.ccfs.se
German / Swedish Chamber of Commerce
www.handelskammer.se
The Dutch Chamber in Sweden
www.dutchchamber.se
Italian Chamber of Commerce
www.italchamber.se

Places to Stay

Short Term Accommodation

If you haven't found accommodation yet and are in need of a roof over your head, there is plenty of short-term accommodation to be had. Here are just a few:

Convendum Living – *www.convendum.se*
Corporate Apartments - *www.bostaddirekt.com*
Apartdirect - *www.apartdirect.com*
Stay Stockholm – *www.staysthlm.com*
Beautiful Apartments – *www.beaps.se*
Företagsbostäder – *www.foretagsbostader.se*
Executive Living – *www.executiveliving.se*

Accomodation and Workspace

Unity in Hammarby Sjöstad combines the unique concept of a home - as well as an office - away from home. They offer fully serviced studio apartments, workspace and facilities such as a café, lounge areas and a gym whilst also arranging workshops and events. Unity Kista Campus near the tech hub of Stockholm in Kista focuses mainly on providing fully furnished studio apartments for students and young professionals.
www.unity-living.com

If you are only here for a short visit, then maybe a hotel would be more comfortable.

Hotels

Amongst the many hotels in Stockholm the historical Grand Hotel is by far the most prestigious and its location couldn't be better, facing the Royal Palace across the water. This historical building was described as 'the listening post of Europe' during the Second World War with the international press setting up their headquarters here, gathering information from both sides, a hub for spies.

Just a hop and a skip away across the bridge on the island of Skeppsholmen lies a somewhat hidden gem, Hotel Skeppsholmen. From their garden terrace you can watch the lively boat traffic and when you are ready for some adventures or sightseeing, just catch the ferry over to Djurgården or Gamla Stan.

Along fashionable Strandvägen you have the unique family-owned Art Nouveau Hotel Diplomat, recognised as Sweden's best hotel by Condé Nast Traveller Magazine for three years in a row. It is a great place for people watching - they also have special relocation offers for monthly stays. Nearby, on Nybrogatan you will find their boutique hotel Villa Dagmar.

In the same area is The Bank on the site of an impressive former bank building - don't miss their rooftop bar 'Le Hibou'! Downtown Camper is the place to be if you want to be active - they offer activities with yoga, kayaking in the Stockholm waters and skateboarding lessons. Their 'Nest' is a rooftop sauna and outdoor pool, open all year round.

These are only a handful of the numerous hotels in the city centre. You will find Mornington Hotel easier on your wallet but perfectly situated in the heart of Östermalm and close to everything! Lastly, let's not forget Ett Hem - it will feel like a home away from home with only 12 rooms and staff catering to your every wish.

Soulful Places

Since the reformation during Gustav Vasa's reign in the 16th century, Sweden has been Protestant. The church of Sweden was part of the Swedish state until 2000. The right to religious freedom is written in the constitution and is quite diverse. Sweden has become increasingly secular and many Swedes seek and find their inner peace through an almost religious relationship with nature. This becomes apparent if you visit the World Heritage Cemetery *Skogskyrkogården* south of Stockholm, where even in death, nature plays an important and fundamental role in the lives of Swedes. Do also visit some of the beautiful churches in Stockholm - many of the churches are used for concerts and musical performances.

St James's Church - *St Jakob*
The red façade and mix of architectural styles of this church really stand out in its central location beside the Opera and Kungsträdgården. It is dedicated to the apostle Saint James the Great, patron saint of travellers. They hold shorter sermons in English as well as concerts several times a week.

The Stockholm Cathedral - *Storkyrkan*
It is in fact called St. Nicholas, but very few Stockholmers know it by this name. *Storkyrkan* in the Old Town is one of the oldest churches in Stockholm, where many a King and Queen have married and been crowned. Check out the fabulous sculpture of St George and the Dragon, sculpted entirely out of oak and antlers commemorating the victory at Brunkeberg against the Danes in 1471.

Also, look for the oil painting *Vädersolstavlan*, hanging on the south wall. Painted in 1636, it is a copy of an original from 1535 and the oldest surviving image of Stockholm.

St Gertrude - *Tyska Kyrkan*
The German church is the second largest church in the Old Town reflecting the close ties Sweden had with Germany during the days of the Hanseatic League. Sermons are held in German. The main core of the building dates back to the late 1500s - look out for the copper gargoyles protruding from the corners of the spire and roof.

Djursholms Kapell
If you happen to be living in Djursholm, do visit Djursholms Kapell atop the hill. It was built in 1898 entirely from donations - the first contributions coming from a group of English Quakers inspired by the influential Louise Woods-Beckman, who lived in Djursholm and was also the brain behind Myrorna (the chain of second-hand shops – now run by the Swedish arm of The Salvation Army). Djursholms Kapell is a popular church to have weddings and christenings in. It is particularly beautiful during the candle-lit service on Christmas Eve.

Hedvig Eleonora
This octagonal church holds a variety of short concerts during the day, or why not join them for their occasional Afternoon Tea. It is centrally located near the Östermalmshallen food hall - step out and listen to the church bells playing different psalms (weekdays at 9am, noon, 3pm, 6pm and 9pm - weekends 9am, 1pm, 3pm, 5pm and 9pm). One of the bells weighs 4.73 tonnes! There are also stunning concerts in the evenings and during the run up to Christmas.

Anglican Church - *Engelska Kyrkan*
St Peter and St Sigfrid's Church, often referred to as the English Church, is an Anglican church in Diplomatstaden near the British Embassy and its residence.
It was originally built in 1866 on Wallingatan in Norrmalm and then under the auspices of Swedish Crown Princess Margaret it was moved 1913, stone by stone, to its current position.
www.stockholmanglicans.se

Catholic Churches

The Catholic diocese of Stockholm consists of 44 parishes all over Sweden. In Stockholm, St Eugenia and St Erik are just some of the many Catholic churches that hold sermons in different languages. To find out where your nearest Catholic church is, check the website.
www.katolskakyrkan.se

Synagogues

The Great Synagogue of Stockholm is located on Wahrendorffsgatan 3 between the Kungsträdgården and Berzelii parks. It is an official national historic building, built in 1870 in an 'oriental' style. The order of service is fairly traditional with the majority of the prayers

in Hebrew and some short sections in Swedish. There are also two orthodox synagogues in Stockholm with a daily minyan - Adat Israel on Södermalm and Adat Jeschurun in the Jewish Centre Bajit in Östermalm.

Mosques

Zayed bin Sultan Al Nahyan's Mosque, more commonly known as the the Stockholm Grand Mosque, is located at Kapellgränd 10 on Södermalm. It was originally designed in 1903 by the well-known architect Ferdinand Boberg to house the electric power station. For more information check their website.
www.stockholmsmoske.se

Shopping

It can be quite disorientating trying to find simple things like a light bulb for sale in Sweden and supermarkets have quite a narrow range. The best place to go is Clas Ohlson which has everything you could possibly want in terms of DIY and house products. Clas Ohlson goes by the name of *gubbdagis* in Sweden and literally means 'fathers' day care centres' - another popular one is Teknikmagasinet with an array of consumer electronics and gadgets. You will need some patience as you need to identify any item you need in their vast catalogues before they will find it for you. Shops also tend to be in shopping centres, so write a good list of what you need to avoid numerous trips.

www.clasohlson.com
www.teknikmagasinet.se

Note that fuses are very different in Sweden to those you may be used to. Some can be bought in local small supermarkets – COOP or ICA – as well as at Clas Ohlson.

Seasonal Essentials
Equally, what you need is very much more defined by season than you may be used to, so here's a checklist. Remember to buy many of these items some time in advance, especially snowsuits, winter boots and Lucia costumes for children as supply is limited.

Winter
- Winter coat made of down (feathers)
- Really sturdy winter boots with good grips
- Rubber studded slip-on grips to put onto boots (*Broddar*)
- Lucia costumes for children
- Snow shovel (in your car as well)
- Ice skates and poles (helmet for kids)
- Ice hockey kit – skates, puck, stick, helmet
- Cross country skis

- Alpine skis & helmets
- Toboggan, preferably a snow racer with steering wheel or try the more affordable *stjärtlapp* or *tefat*
- Studded tyres for bike

Spring

- Light down jacket
- Sunglasses
- Bike (lightweight as Stockholm is quite hilly, or tougher for cross-country)

Summer
- Boating shoes
- Kayak or inflatable canoe (can also be rented)
- Tent
- Portable barbeque
- Prongs for cooking sausages
- Lifejackets
- Red trousers (to show you've sailed the Atlantic, if you have!)

Autumn
- Bilberry and/or lingonberry pickers
- Mushroom guidebook (available from Natural History Museum). There are also apps you can download such as: Mushroom Identify - Automatic picture recognition
- Waterproof suits for children
- Winter tyres for car
- Organise the rental of a boat for next summer!

Your Personal Number & Benefits

Personnummer

Although we generally prefer to be known by name, rather than as a number, getting your *personnummer* in Sweden is an absolutely crucial first step. Without this, you cannot get a job, pay tax, receive benefits, get a mobile phone contract, join any organisation with subscriptions. It really is your gateway to all these things and although rather arduous, should be taken care of as soon as possible.

You will need to go to the Swedish tax authority – *Skatteverket* – with specific documents as explained on their website. If you go to their website and type in the search box 'moving to Sweden - civil registration' this will all be explained.
www.skatteverket.se

Once you are successfully registered, you will be formally registered as living at a particular address and on the Swedish Population Register. You should carry your personal number with you at all times, as you will be asked for it frequently. As it is connected with everything you do, don't be surprised if people seem to know a lot about you, particularly your age which forms part of the 12-digit code!

Swedish Social Insurance

As a general rule, you must either formally reside in Sweden or be employed and work here to be eligible for social security benefits.

The child allowance is SEK 1,250 per child/month and if you have more than one child, as an extra perk for being a prolific child bearer you will receive an additional SEK 150/month for every extra child. This is paid until the child is 16.

Other benefits include a parental allowance which is paid to the mother or father for 16 months after the child is born (whilst retaining your job). The parental allowance may be divided equally between the parents, except for 90 days' for each parent which cannot be transferred. An increasing number of stay-at-home fathers choose to take over childcare once the mother returns to work. Children are guaranteed a place in daycare from the age of 12 months and part of the parental allowance can also be saved and taken out until the child turns 8.

If you are working in Sweden, you will soon become familiar with the word VAB (*vård av barn*), when someone stays at home from work to look after their sick child. They will then receive VAB-compensation from *Försäkringskassan*.

February in Sweden seems to be the month when many children fall ill and *februari* is thus sometimes referred to as *vabruari*.

Pets

When visiting or travelling to Sweden you can bring your dog, cat or other animal if they fulfil certain EU rules. There are common requirements for travelling with dogs or cats within the EU.

Once you have arrived in Sweden with your pet there are some important rules to be aware of. All dogs and cats must be chipped, vaccinated against rabies and reported to customs when passing the border.

Your dog should be let outside at least every 6 hours. If you keep it indoors, there must be a window providing sunlight. Your dog should be on a lead at all times unless you are in the forest - however from the 1st March to 20th August they must be on the lead in the forest too, as there are new-born animals there. You must always clear up after your dogs and dispose of bags in rubbish bins provided.

More information can be found on the Swedish Board of Agriculture website:
jordbruksverket.se

In case of emergency, there is a Veterinary Hospital called *Djurakuten* in the city on Kungstensgatan 58 or another animal hospital in Albano near Stockholm University.
www.djurakuten.se
www.anicura.se

Food

Savouring another country's food can be one of the most rewarding parts of living abroad. It can also make you feel completely disorientated, as key ingredients are noticeably lacking from the shelves, meat is prepared in another way, everything tastes 20% different to how it did when you cooked it at home, or you just can't find what you need.

Broadly speaking, Sweden's diet is dominated by fish - predominantly salmon (*lax*), herrings (*sill* or *strömming*) and prawns (*räkor*) – potatoes, bread which comes in a vast number of varieties and of which sourdough and sweetened brown malt bread are the most delicious, muesli seemingly of a million varieties, sausages also of a million varieties (of which the round red *falukorv* shouldn't be missed), crispbread (*knäckebröd*) which comes in enormous flat, crisp round circles and cakes. Swedish cakes and buns are wonderful and offer a cornucopia of choices showcasing the Swedes' love of using exotic spices in baking.

It's noticeable that Swedes also have foreign food fads. Tex Mex food is still popular in many circles – every Swede knows about 'Taco Friday'! Italian food is deeply revered and some foreign influences (*kåldolmar*) date back to the 1600s when King Karl XII spent many years in the Ottoman Empire.

Other food, such as Indian, is largely unrepresented, while sushi exerts the same fascination as in other countries. You will find a dizzying choice of lactose as well as gluten free products available. Like the Dutch, Scandinavians in general are unusually lactose tolerant compared to southern Europeans. However, Swedes have become increasingly gluten intolerant - there are theories about why this might be and some believe it could be owing to high consumption of välling (a gruel given to babies but also popular amongst some adults) during the 1980s when gluten presumably was added to it.

Mirroring the Swedish adoration of particular festivals, there are special dishes or cakes which are synonymous with these occasions and take on importance of mythical proportions. Enjoying these is an absolute delight and will give you a real in-road into feeling part of Sweden's cherished celebrations. The Christmas *Julbord* is a unique set piece – you will work your way through many courses of different delicacies. It's essential to remain open-minded and pace yourself! You may find many Swedish foods either very salty or sweet. The combination of saltiness as well as the sweetness comes from the old method of food preservation and is a combination frequently found in Swedish foods. For instance, when curing the salmon for *gravad lax* you use equal amounts of salt and sugar.

Here is a list of food you shouldn't miss (recipes for those with an asterisk can be found at the end of the book):

> ***Kanelbullar*** (cinnamon buns) – utterly delectable, these can come in reasonable, or epic sizes and the sheer waft of warm cinnamon will never cease to seduce.

> ***Kardemummabulle*** (cardamon bun) – another delicious bun with the distinct taste of cardamon.

> ***Kladdkaka*** (chocolate cake) – gorgeously gooey and quietly decadent, this is a staple amongst Swedish cakes and irresistible.

> ***Semla*** bun, *semlor*, *fastlagsbullar* or *fettisdagsbullar* – a yeasty bun filled with lashings of whipped cream and almond paste, traditionally eaten during Lent but now available pretty much as soon as Christmas is over. On the 7th Tuesday before Easter you will be lucky to get away with eating just one of these buns - it is *Semmeldagen*.

Truffel (chocolate truffles) – these come at a shocking price in cafés as an afterthought to lunch but are a real indulgence. Think of a sharp cocoa hit per mouthful.

Chokladboll - every Swedish child can make these rich chocolate balls and they are found in practically every cake shop.

Prinsesstårta – not for the faint-hearted, this bright green, marzipan covered cake is a sequence of layers of light sponge, jam and indulgent cream.

Räksmörgås – sandwiches are piled high with handfuls of sweet, pink prawns and then piled a bit higher for good measure. These sandwiches are usually open and the quality seems universally superb. For larger celebrations you may even come upon the traditional *Smörgårtårta* - a huge layered sandwich cake!

Janssons frestelse (Janssons temptation) – a reassuringly salty version of *pommes dauphinoise*, where anchovies (make sure to get the Swedish kind) offset the creaminess of layered potatoes, cream and butter.

Köttbullar (meatballs) – you either love them or you hate them, but they will be on almost every menu you will ever come across in Sweden and always served with lingonberries (themselves a rather bitter, acquired taste but loved by the Swedes and served with many different meats).

Pannkakor (pancakes) – the childhood staple, served with lashings of whipped cream and generous dollops of raspberry jam. Essential when skiing, or just warming up on a winter's day.

Sill (herring) – a real test for the newcomer and offered in a myriad of cures, the fish being pickled in vinegar accompanied by an array of spices. Those with cream and dill are more forgiving to the inexperienced palette, as are those prepared in honeyed mustard sauce.

Lax (salmon) – salmon is a law unto itself in Sweden, prepared at various stages of smoking, cured or simply poached. The most popular version is *gravad lax** - cured salmon served with a delicious, sweet mustard sauce, fresh potatoes and dill. Try our cured salmon recipe with the mustard sauce*.

Kalix Löjrom (bleak or vendace roe) - sometimes referred to as the 'Gold of the Bothnian Bay'. It should be eaten accompanied by finely chopped red onion, sour cream and bread fried in butter.

Senap (mustard) – this comes in many forms, but those with generous quantities of honey (*honung*) are absolutely delicious and terribly moreish with just about anything.

Kantarell (chanterelles) – these mushrooms are exquisite and enthusiastically gathered by Swedes in every forest during the autumn. *kantarellsoppa* (soup) is heavenly and dried chanterelles are a fantastic staple for the store cupboard – just soften them in boiling water, chop and add to creamy sauces for a real depth of flavour. There are two main varieties of *kantareller* – the orange coloured delicacy and then the poorer cousin *trattkantarell* but both are worthy excuses for a mushroom hunt!

Falukorv - a big sausage that you normally slice and eat pan fried or cooked in the oven. The main ingredients are beef and pork with potato starch, onion and seasoning. The sausage is pre-cooked in a red plastic casing (which you remove before cooking) and shaped into a round ring. It has an interesting history, originating from the northern town of Falun. In Falun in the Dalarna region, there was a big copper mining industry. Ox hide was used for making ropes used in the mines, meaning there was a surplus of meat which was often salted and smoked – thus the *falukorv* was born!

Some Swedish foods will really put hairs on your chest and shouldn't be missed if you want to call yourself a real Swedish Viking - the traditional *lutfisk* for Christmas and *surströmming* on the third Thursday in August, as well as *Kalles kaviar* or *messmör* on your toast for breakfast.

Kalles kaviar is a cod roe paste, while *messmör* is a paste made from whey (a milk protein) - both come in tubes!

Lutfisk is dried and salted cod pickled in lye (sodium hydroxide). After having been rehydrated for days it is then cooked in the oven (or microwave oven). When served it is slightly gelatinous in texture and translucent and goes tremendously well with small boiled peas, boiled potatoes, melted butter and a white sauce.

Surströmming is a small Baltic herring caught in the spring, salted and left to ferment before being canned. The fermentation process continues in the tin, resulting in a bulging tin of fermented herring. The aroma is really pungent but the taste is surprisingly rounded - the fish is served on a hard bread or in a roll of soft flat bread together with boiled potatoes, sour cream and onions. The fermentation originates from a lactic acid enzyme in the fish's spine. NEVER open a tin of *surströmming* indoors!

Some foreign ingredients are tricky, or impossible to find in Swedish supermarkets. You will need to make your own self-raising flour, for instance – see the recipe at the end of the book – and it can also be difficult to find ground almonds.

If you are Dutch, you may find yourself missing specialties such as *Hagelslag*, *Appelstroop*, *Stroopwafels* and *Pepernoten* around the *Sinterklaas* celebration. And if you're German, you may miss Milka chocolate and Gummi bears, typical German gingerbread – *Lebkuchen* – around Christmas, as well as a goose for the festival of St. Martin in November.

However, help is at hand, as Lidl tends to stock some German specialities and there is a Dutch cheese shop in Stockholm. Americans can stock up on favourite treats at the American Food and Gift Store at Sveavägen 106 or in Täby Centrum, and those yearning for wonderful French patisseries can head to La Petite France at John Ericssonsgatan 6 on Kungsholmen. If you have run out of Marmite head for Gamla Stan and the Little Britain Shop on Lilla Nygatan 11. You can also find quite a good range of Asian foods in small food shops around Hötorget.

www.littlebritainshop.se
www.englishshop.se
www.gamla-amsterdam.se
www.theamericanfoodandgiftstore.se
www.petitefrance.se

The Swedish *Julbord*

Since we are on the topic of food, everyone has heard of the *Smörgåsbord* and if ever there was the ultimate *Smörgåsbord* it would be the Christmas *Julbord*, served in most restaurants from the beginning of November. If you happen to be working at a Swedish company, you will probably be invited to enjoy at least one. This is not just a buffet of everyday foods - it is full of family traditions, some fairly normal dishes as well as some more unusual local specialties, so be prepared to try all of it. Some of the standard *Julbord* dishes include pickled herring, cured salmon, ham, meatballs, small sausages (*prinskorv*), Janssons temptation (a delicious concoction of potatoes, cream and anchovies), ribs, pâtés, beetroot salad, a variety of cabbage dishes, cheeses and bread. Then you have the specialities:

> **Grisfötter** - Pigs trotters – not always a favourite!

> **Dopp i grytan** – dipping bread into the stock in which the ham was cooked. This has long been a tradition; thus Christmas eve in Sweden is often referred to as '*doppare dan*' - the dipping day!

> **Kalvsylta** – Jellied veal

> **Lutfisk** – A gelatinous white fish served with a lot of accompaniments (as mentioned earlier)

> **Ål** - smoked eel (fishing eel is highly regulated in Sweden as the eel is on the verge of extinction)

The Christmas table is often decorated with a gingerbread house, lots of candles and sometimes a pig's head with an apple in its mouth (not the most appetising of table decorations). For pudding/dessert there will be a variety of sweets/candies such as marzipan figures, *sega tomtar* (chewy Father Christmases), *marmelad* squares, *kola* (soft and hard toffees), *is-choklad* (hardened chocolate with coconut oil), as well as *ris à la Malta* (rice pudding with jam) or *saftsås* (sweet sauce), *mandelmusslor* (a delicate almond cake topped with whipped cream and jam), *klenäter* (deep fried pastry), *pepparkakor* (ginger biscuits), dates, figs and nuts.

To drink, you warm up with *glögg* (by now you will have had enough *glögg* to last you until next year!). You will be served some *aquavit* or *snaps* with your food, together with some type of Christmas beer or homemade *mumma* and *Julmust* for the children. The traditional song to accompany the *snaps* is:

Hej Tomtegubbar
Hej, tomtegubbar, slå i glasen
Och låt oss lustiga vara!
Hej, tomtegubbar, slå i glasen
Och låt oss lustiga vara!
En liten tid vi leva här, med
Mycket möda och stort besvär.
Hej, tomtegubbar, slå i glasen.
Och låt oss lustiga vara!

Translation:
Hey, all ye Santas, fill your glasses and let's be jolly together.
Hey, all ye Santas, fill your glasses and let's be jolly together.
Our time is brief upon the earth, with lots of trouble and little mirth.
Hey, all ye Santas, fill your glasses and let's be jolly together.

Drink & Alcohol

Sweden and its Scandinavian counterparts sell alcohol in a uniquely controlled way, through a state monopoly. In Sweden, all alcohol is sold by government run shops called *Systembolaget*, which can be found in all towns and throughout cities. They are extremely well stocked with a superb choice of wines, beer and spirits – it is said that *Systembolaget* is one of the largest individual purchasers of alcohol in the world and hence the quality and range of what it sells is excellent.

Whereas going to buy alcohol previously had a stigma attached to it in Sweden, *Systembolaget* is now very sophisticated and you will be offered advice as to how to match wine with what you are cooking. It also stocks *glögg* aplenty in the festive season – this is a staple of Christmas, should be served warmed with almonds and raisins, and warms you to the very heart.

The sale of Coca Cola plummets during the festive season while children delight in their own Christmas drink, *Julmust,* an intensely sweet, very dark concoction which forms the perfect accompaniment to watching *Kalle Anka's Julafton* (Donald Duck) on television on Christmas Eve. This is how you will find many a good Swede occupied at 3 o'clock before Father Christmas comes knocking on the door.

You will also find a wide variety of traditional alcoholic drinks such as *Julöl* (Christmas beer), *Mumma* (a blend of sweetened beer and stout with a taste of cardamom) as well as *snaps, nubbe* or *aquavit* (alcohol distilled from grain or potatoes, possibly spiced with an endless variety of natural flavours). S*naps, nubbe* or *aquavit* accompany most celebrations such as Christmas, Midsummer and the *kräftskiva* (crayfish) parties in August.

An unwritten rule is that you never drink these fiery offerings without singing. You will need to learn at least one traditional Swedish drinking song, but you may also like to have your own short drinking song up your sleeve in case you are asked to perform – you will suddenly be surrounded by extrovert performers casting aside their guise of Swedish shyness! Here is one of the most common drinking songs (also written phonetically):

Helan Går (in Swedish)
Helan går, sjung hopp fader Allan
lallan lej
Helan går, sjung hopp fader Allan lej

Och den som inte helan tar
han heller inte halvan får;
Helan går!
Sjung hopp fader Allan lej

Hell and Gore (phonetic)
Hell and gore
Chung Hop father Allan lallan Lay
Hell and gore
Chung Hop father Allan Lay

Oh handsome in the hell and tar
and hell are in a half and four
Hell and goooooore!
Chung Hop father Allan Ley

The absolutely key thing to remember about *Systembolaget* is its opening times. It closes early on a Saturday afternoon and is closed all day on Sunday and on public holidays. Details can be found on their website to avoid thirsty disappointment!

www.systembolaget.se

Food Shopping

Sweden has a good range of supermarkets, the most prominent being COOP, ICA, Willys, Lidl, City Gross and Hemköp. ICA Maxi is the larger supermarket of the ICA chain. In terms of good value shops / stores, you will also find Lidl and sometimes Willys. Supermarkets range from enormous ones in retail shopping parks beside motorways, to smaller supermarkets in smaller sized shopping centres or local, convenience versions in city centres or towns.

Around Stockholm, you will find large supermarkets at Arninge, Täby, Kungens Kurva, Mall of Scandinavia, Bromma Blocks etc. It is very easy to order online too, with both home deliveries and click and collect / pick-up and delivery available. Amazon.se was launched in October 2020, so ordering from here is now simple too. You will receive a written notification, email or SMS that a package has arrived. Pick up points are usually in your nearby grocery store - ask your neighbour where it is and don't forget to bring along your ID card or passport!

There are some hot spots for food shopping in Stockholm. Saluhallen on Östermalmstorg is one of these, being Stockholm's ancient meat and fish market dating from the 1880s. It is somewhere to feast your eyes, meet a friend for *fika* or a light lunch, or splash out on something from the array of wonderful fish of every description, shellfish, meat (including beef, reindeer, venison as well as cured meats), cakes, jams, wild mushrooms and  beautifully crafted take-away meals of the highest quality. Some people order their Christmas ham from there too – start saving now! *www.ostermalmshallen.se*

If you are yearning for a British sausage, go no further than Taylors & Jones at Hantverkargatan 12 on Kungsholmen. Their sausages are legendary! Or if you'd like to see typical Swedish stripy sugar canes being made by hand, visit the *Polkagriskokeri* at Stora Nygatan 44 in Gamla Stan and be treated to a live display of extraordinary craftsmanship.

Taylor & Jones - *www.taylorsandjones.com*
Polkagris in Gamla Stan - *www.gamlastanspolkagriskokeri.se*

Markets and food halls
Leading department store NK has recently reopened its new food hall on the lower ground floor. Hötorget has an excellent vegetable market, which is replaced by a flea market on Sundays. Underground by the vegetable market you will find Hötorgshallen (Haymarkethall), a food hall where you can enjoy food from all over the world and buy Turkish hamburgers, traditional Swedish Toast Skagen as well as delicacies from Italy to Peru.
www.hotorgshallen.se

Several outdoor markets open especially for Christmas - you can find these on Stortorget in Gamla Stan and Sergels Torg, as well as the Christmas market at Skansen. These normally sell speciality Christmas foods (gingerbread, saffron rolls and *glögg*) as well as decorations. Father Christmas's – *tomtar* – feature particularly prominently! Many local squares have smaller vegetable markets during the warmer months.

Going to the Supermarket

This can be both a daunting and exciting experience, as the emphasis on particular foods may be very different to what you are used to and you will need to become familiar with some very precise vocabulary to be sure of finding what you're looking for.

Unless you have applied for a 'self-scan' service at one of the large supermarkets, the fruit and vegetables are weighed by the cashier.

A number of different terms are used to give information about products:

- ***Extrapris*** means that the price has been temporarily reduced.
- ***Kort datum*** means that the product's expiry date has almost been reached. Sometimes stores sell these products at reduced prices.
- ***Bäst Före*** means best before and indicates that the date printed on the product is the recommended date for the product's consumption.
- ***Ekologiskt*** means that the product is organic and has been grown/produced without artificial pesticides or hormones.
- ***Bra miljöval*** means that the product has been certified as having a low impact on the environment (for its product category). The products are marked with a green and white logo with a stylised swan.

There are also numerous varieties of staple products which you may not be familiar with – in any case, it's crucial to know the right word!

Flour
- Graham / Wholemeal flour - *Grahamsmjöl*
- Oats - *Havregryn*
- Rye - *Råg*

- Wheat flour/White flour – *Vetemjöl*

Types of sugar
- Brown sugar - *Farinsocker*
- Icing sugar/Powdered sugar - *Florsocker*
- Golden syrup - *Ljus sirap*
- Granulated white sugar - *Strösocker*
- Molasses - *Mörk Sirap/Baksirap*
- Sugar cubes - *Bitsocker*

Bread, biscuits and crispbreads
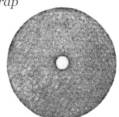
- French loaf/white bread - *Franska*
- Wholegrain - *Fullkorn*
- Cookies (Sweet) - *Kakor*
- Crackers - *Kex*
- Crisp bread, - *Knäckebröd* In the old times they were baked round with a hole in the middle and stored on sticks under the roof. These can still be bought in the supermarkets.
- Rusks - *Skorpor*
- Thin flat unleavened bread (soft/hard), traditional for northern Sweden - *Tunnbröd (mjukt/hårt)*
- Wort flavoured rye bread – *Vörtlimpa*

Miscellaneous
- Almond - *Mandel*
- Baking powder - *Bakpulver*
- Dry yeast - *Torrjäst*
- Fresh/Live yeast - *Kronjäst* (red text for sweet bread)
- Hazelnuts - *Hasselnötter*
- Peanuts - *Jordnötter*
- Vanilla custard - *Vaniljsås/Marsansås*
- Walnut - *Valnöt*

Buying dairy products can be a significant challenge as there are a multitude of options and some things you are unlikely to have seen before, as well as an incredible choice of lactose-free products. Here are some tips:

Butter (*Smör*) & Margarine (*Margarin*)
Butter for spreading on bread is sold in boxes with a lid and comes with different percentages of fat with added salt - Flora and Bregott are the most common makes. The fat (usually butter and rapeseed oil) levels are often graded where full fat (75-80%) is standard. The percentages should be clearly visible on the box. Here is just an example of the different types of Bregott that you can find on the shelves (Note: they are all salted!):

- Bregott *normalsaltat* (normally salted)
- Bregott *mellan* (medium salted)
- Bregott *extra saltat* (extra salted)
- Bregott *ekologisk brynt* (browned and salted)
- Bregott *havsalt* (sea salt)

Paper-wrapped pats of butter marked *smör* are so-called 'real butter'. This has not been processed for use on sandwiches and is therefore quite hard and usually used for baking and cooking. Unsalted butter can be found but sometimes you may have to ask for it. You can also find paper-wrapped (usually larger) pieces of margarine.

Cheese (*Ost*)
Certainly not of French, or even English proportions, Sweden's range of cheese is mostly hard and uncomplicated, differing in flavour, fat content and style. *Hushållsost* is a mild cheese, *herrgårdsost* and *prästost* are usually medium and *grevé* and *västerbottensost* are the stronger kinds, the latter being widely used in punchy cheese tarts.

Each type of cheese also has milder and stronger versions. *Lagrad* (which means matured) often means that it has a little more flavour, *vällagrad* or *extralagrad* means that it is very flavoursome. The normal (and cheaper) way of buying cheese is in one piece rather than in slices.

A utensil called an *osthyvel* (cheese slicer or cheese planer) is used to slice the cheese at home. Cottage cheese is called *keso* and can be found in the milk and butter counter. A Swedish speciality called *messmör* or *fjällbrynt* is a sweet soft spreadable cheese with high iron and calcium content.

Check out the tubed cheeses!

Milk (*Mjölk*)

The different types of milk are *lättmjölk* (light/low fat) which usually comes in a yellow or light blue carton, *mellanmjölk* (medium fat content) in a green carton and *mjölk* (the highest fat content) in a red carton. Take care not to confuse the cartons with similarly coloured cartons of *filmjölk*, which are often on the same shelf. These contain an unsweetened yogurt or sour milk style product commonly eaten with breakfast cereal. If you want to use milk in cooking, for vital things such as pancakes, be sure to use full fat milk to achieve the taste you are looking for.

Sour Cream

There are two sour cream style products - *crème fraiche* and *gräddfil*. *Crème fraiche* has a range of fat contents and additional flavourings and can be used for cooking. *Gräddfil* is not as thick and is often used for dressings or dips – it will curdle if cooked!

Yoghurt (yogurt)

Conveniently, yogurt has the same name in Swedish as in English. There is a dizzying assortment of yogurt products with a host of different flavours, fat and sugar contents. You can also buy cooking yogurt (*matlagningsyoghurt*), Turkish yogurt (*Turkisk yogurt*) and Greek yogurt (*Grekisk yogurt*) by the bucketful - literally.

Other yoghurts

Onaka is a yoghurt popular in Japan, boasting special probiotic bacteria. *Lantfil, A-fil* and *långfil* are all types of lighter, less sour yoghurt which can make a good combination with muesli. They come in a variety of flavours.

Fish & Seafood

Where would the Scandinavian diet be without fish? 90% of the salmon consumed in Sweden is imported from Norway and is cheaper than the wild salmon from Sweden. You will find a superb choice with salmon, herring and prawns of all shapes and sizes featuring prominently. You should also be prepared to experiment with some very smoky and salty varieties. Have plenty of refreshing water or beer at the ready! Here are some of the main options you will find on offer and you should ask for *bitar/skivor* (slices each large enough for one person) at the counter:

- *Flundra* – flounder (flat, saltwater fish)
- *Lax* - salmon (can be sold fresh, frozen, smoke-cured/*rökt* or raw spice-cured/*gravad*)
- *Röding* – charr (cold water fish, similar to salmon)
- *Sej* – coalfish (otherwise known as pollock)
- *Sill* - herring from the west coast (mostly sold in glass jars. The herring is pickled and comes in different flavours and sauces)

- *Strömming* - Baltic herring, often fried
- *Torsk* - cod
- *Kräftor* - crayfish
- *Musslor* - mussels/clams
- *Räkor* - shrimps or prawns (*ishavsräkor* - shrimps from the Arctic Ocean are a particular speciality)

Fruits

Summer fruits in Sweden are treated with true reverence, embodying as they do the Swedish adoration of things in season, nature and being reminiscent of some of Sweden's most charming children's books including those by Elsa Beckow. Markets and shops will offer very expensive, but delicious small boxes of blueberries, strawberries and raspberries, whilst their bitterer counterparts – the lingonberry and cloudberry – will be used as foils to rich gamey meat, meatballs and Christmas offerings. Here are some key fruity words:

- *Blåbär* - blueberry
- *Citron* - lemon
- *Fläder* - elder (berry or leaf - cordial is often made from leaves and flowers from the elder bush)
- *Hallon* - raspberry

- *Hjortron* - cloudberry (a northern speciality)
- *Smultron* – wild strawberry
- *Jordgubbe* - strawberry
- *Lingon* - lingonberry/red whortleberry

Vegetables

Sweden's do-it-yourself where it comes to vegetables consists of a limited, hard core of root vegetables. These are simply what grow well in such a challenging climate as those who keep their heads below the ground have the advantage - this explains the ubiquitous appearance of beetroot salad with grilled goat's cheese on so many restaurant menus. The quality of vegetables sourced from further afield can vary enormously, often simply as a function of the time taken for them to be transported by lorry in freezing conditions from key ports such as Rotterdam. So in winter, you may be in for some disappointing samples of tender green vegetables and herbs, with many a basil wilting in its pot. However, the Swedish determination to eat what's more exotic as well as homespun means that there is a continued good variety of vegetables, even if they're not necessarily at their best all year round. Here are some of the Swedish stalwarts. Horseradish often features as an excellent foil to prawns when mixed with some crème fraiche.

- *Majs* - corn/maize
- *Morot* - carrot
- *Palsternacka* - parsnip
- *Pepparrot* - horseradish
- *Purjolök* - leek
- *Rotselleri* - celeriac

- *Vitkål* - cabbage
- *Vitlök* - garlic
- *Ärtor* - peas

Meat

Sweden has an excellent range of meat with a distinct commitment in restaurants to sourcing really good quality, locally farmed meat – with prices to match! There is a real dedication to producing excellent meat, as evidenced by the use of antibiotics in feedstuff having been banned in 1986.

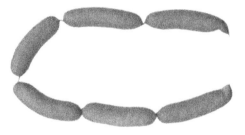

There are also plenty of game options for the adventurous which range from interesting to delicious. You might think twice before offering your children reindeer, as it does tend to taint idyllic images of Christmas, but then when in Rome...... As for sausages, the range is seemingly unending and can be nothing short of traumatic, depending on your taste for or aversion to quite rubbery offerings. But let's be open-minded – they are ready in a jiffy as they are pre-cooked and only need a quick warm-through. There are also barbecues on hand in many of Sweden's forests and walking spots, as well as on the ski slopes, where you can warm said sausages and consume with gusto.

When buying meat, chicken and pork are definitely the more affordable options, whilst beef and lamb are a notch up in terms of expense.

Key meaty vocabulary is below:

- *Fläsk* - pork
- *Hjort* - venison
- *Kalkon* - turkey
- *Kalv* - veal
- *Kyckling* - chicken
- *Nöt* - beef
- *Ren* - reindeer
- *Vilt* - assorted game
- *Älg* – moose
- *Blandfärs* - minced pork and beef
- *Blodpudding* - blood pudding/black pudding (made from pig's blood)
- *Falukorv* - a type of pork sausage
- *Isterband* - spiced sausage-like product made from the fattier pieces of pork (*ister*=fat)
- *Kassler* - boneless smoked pork chops
- *Korv* - sausage (sausages usually contain pork, unless specified otherwise)
- *Köttfärs/Nötfärs* - minced beef

Restaurants

There are any number of restaurants in Stockholm, of which we only mention a few. The range of cuisine available has increased hugely in recent years and the city now has a really excellent, very high-quality restaurant scene. These are some of the classic ones, well known to most Swedes and frequented by them. When you are out eating with Swedish friends, don't be surprised if you split the bill or pay for exactly what you have eaten and drunk. Swedes generally do not like to feel indebted to anyone – again, the ever-independent Swede! And to be honest, eating out feels like a vast expense so you won't want to pay for more than you've had. This is why it's a mercy that the quality of food is so good, but this is likely to be a real event, rather than something you do all the time. It is the alcohol which really breaks the camel's back.

 Eating out at lunchtime is an entirely different matter and you will often get a good-sized meal at a reasonable price. Thursdays you may find pea soup (*ärtsoppa*) on the menu – this is traditionally eaten with a huge dollop of sweet mustard. In the evening the soup will be accompanied by a glass of warm *Punsch* - a very sweet alcoholic liqueur tasting of arrack. There are of course, drinking songs for this drink as well.

If you are in a restaurant or at a bar and you order spirits, shots or aquavit (*snaps*), the waiter may ask if you want fours (normal) or sixes (large). These are the measurements used by bartenders to measure out the alcohol in the glass i.e. 4 centilitres (40ml/1.4 fl.oz) or 6 centilitres (60ml/2 fl.oz) - it will never randomly be poured out into the glass.

It's also worth mentioning that Swedes are extremely organised when it comes to eating out, so don't imagine that you can be spontaneous, simply drop in on a restaurant at the weekend and find a table with ease. You will need to think ahead and reserve! This almost always takes place online, as restaurants have very sophisticated booking platforms on their websites.

Sturehof
If you want to experience a restaurant where seafood is a key feature in the menu, this is the place to go. It has a genuine atmosphere and is situated bang in the middle of Stockholm, close to the city's nightlife. This is also one of the two restaurants where you can try the infamous *surströmming* once a year - if you are up to it!
www.sturehof.com

Prinsen
Since 1897, Prinsen has served traditional Swedish foods such as Biff Rydberg and Wallenbergare, not forgetting Swedish meatballs. A cosy atmosphere with good food.
www.restaurangprinsen.se

Grodan
Another classic and originally named *La Grenouille* - this name didn't stick, so was changed to the colloquial *Grodan*, Swedish for frog. They serve a good mix of French and Swedish cuisine.

KB (*Konstnärsbaren*)
Konstnärsbaren (the Artist Bar) in Konstnärshuset (the Artist House) is also situated in Östermalm - it is a beautiful building worthy of a closer look on Smålandsgatan. Inside is a unique milieu created by the Stockholm artist community.

Berns
Don't miss a visit to this beautiful historical building overlooking Berzelii park on Nybroplan. It was built as a palace of entertainment for Stockholmers in 1863 and still is. This was also the first restaurant in Sweden to serve Asian food and this is still very much a theme on their menu.

Ulla Winbladh
This is another favourite amongst Stockholmers on Djurgården. It was built in 1897 and named after one of composer Carl Michael Bellman's muses. They have a great *Julbord* during winter and, weather permitting, a large terrace outside during the summer. They serve traditional Swedish food.

Ulriksdals Värdshus
This is also famous for its *Julbord* in November and December. A 19th century wooden inn overlooking the gardens and lake by Ulriksdals Palace.

Stallmästaregården
Another old inn located just off Royal Haga Park and Brunnsviken. It is famous for its *Julbord* and you can also stay overnight in their intimate boutique hotel.

Pelikan
Don't miss a visit to this famous Stockholm building on Södermalm with its old beer hall and historic interior. It used to be the southernmost outpost before leaving the city of Stockholm. You can order their famous *Grosshandlarmiddag* (wholesalers' dinner) which will keep you going for days!

Gondolen

At the time of writing, we understand that Gondolen will reopen in 2022 after major renovation. It is situated 33 metres above ground in the iconic landmark *Katarinahissen* (Katarina Elevator) overlooking Slussen on Södermalm. This is an opening we are looking forward to as the views are fantastic - either have a drink at the bar or indulge in a stupendous meal!

Kvarnen

Also on Södermalm, at Kvarnen you can indulge in traditional Swedish food and beer. The word *kvarnen* means mill and this is where they began to spin! In 1908 the building was adapted to house a restaurant. The interior of today's Kvarnen reflects how a typical restaurant might have looked at that time.

Eating in Djursholm

If you are based in or around Djursholm, there are a number of good restaurants to try. Monrad's has long been the place to eat in Djursholm, with very high quality food and a particular focus on very fresh fish, which is also sold in the delicatessen. Monrad's also provides a catering service. Other excellent options include Brasserie Greta which, as the name suggests, has a French focus with good brasserie-style food. If you want to go Italian, try la Piazza, which has delicious pasta, risotto and meat specialities such as *saltimbocca*.
www.monrads.se
www.brasseriegreta.se
www.lapiazzadjursholm.se

Other options by the water include Café Ekudden, which is opposite Villa Pauli (the country members' club) on Strandvägen in Djursholm, which makes a very pretty spot to watch the boats between you and Lidingö on summer afternoons. Over on Tranholmen – a fascinating island reached only by boat in summer and footbridge in winter – you can dine at the hands of a chef in his own home. David@home is a wonderful experience – intimate and definitely different. Or further towards Stockholm, Bockholmen is a gorgeous restaurant in a stunning pale yellow house with lawns tumbling down to the waterside, where you can moor your boat if

approaching that way! This is a real treat in summer, but also cosy in winter. Don't miss it!
www.davidathome.se
www.bockholmen.com

Eating on Lidingö
If you want to experience all the charm of an old country inn visit Långängensgård in Lidingö's nature reserve. This can be combined with long walks in the surrounding woods. Nearby, you will find Kottla lake where there is a great café Vattenverket on the lakefront amongst the trees. It is open daily (9-5) with comfortable seating both in and out!
www.langangensgard.se
www.vattenverket.se

If you crave for some American fastfood then head to Herserudsvägen 1 and you will get your fill at American Taste Away. Further out on the island is the Elfvik Farm with a nice café and also Elfviks gård built 1775 where you can enjoy a great brunch. If you want an overnight stay combining a good meal with a spa experience, check out the newly opened Ellery Beach Hotel!
www.elfviksgard.nu
americantasteaway.com
www.elfviksherrgard.se

Eating in Nacka Strand
If you want a short boat trip out in the Stockholm archipelago combined with a lunch or dinner, then take the SL-boat from Nybroplan. Get off at Nacka strand – here you have an array of choices such as Restaurant J, Funky Chicken Food Truck, Savör, Forna Romano, Miss Goong, Restaurang Heat and last but not least the Little Britain Tea Garden. A small picturesque café serving fresh hot scones with clotted cream and tea – they also have a small shop. Check their website to make sure they are open before venturing up the steep steps. Their tables are spread out on the cliff overlooking the inlet to Stockholm – one of the best vantage points for boat spotting! (not to be missed).
www.littlebritainteagarden.se

The Best *Fika*

Swedes have a longstanding tradition of drinking coffee and breaking up the working day with *fika* - this normally entails having a cup of very strong coffee with something sweet to go with it. You are expected to join your colleagues for *fika* –it will give you the chance to get to know them in a more informal way.

Coffee first arrived in Sweden in the 17th century. In 1746, a royal decree was issued and coffee was heavily taxed, before being actually banned. This didn't stop the Swedes from buying coffee on the black market. In 1820 the ban on coffee was finally lifted and coffee drinking sky-rocketed.

Sweden's take on coffee chains consists chiefly of Espresso House or Wayne's Coffee. Café Gateaux, Fabrique and Bröd & Salt are bakeries with good quality bread and buns. There are any number of places in Stockholm where you can enjoy a good cup of coffee with a traditional bun - here are just some of our favourites:

Grillska Huset – Stortorget, Gamla Stan
When you are out sightseeing in the Old Town we would highly recommend stopping for *fika* here. The café and small bakery next door are run by Stadsmissionen (founded in 1853) and have been here for more than 100 years with proceeds going to those in need. If you visit the bakery don't forget to look up at their beautiful ceiling. They have won the prestigious prize for the best *semla* several years running. In summer there is a charming terrace at the back of the café where you can sit in the sun. So why not support a good cause while indulging in a delicious *kardemummabulle*?!

Chokladkoppen – Stortorget, Gamla Stan
Chokladkoppen is a cosy café in one of the unique buildings in the square at the heart of Gamla Stan. They are famous for their hot chocolate which Jamie Oliver raved about when visiting Stockholm. This is also a gay-friendly café where you can catch up with the latest upcoming gay events.

Tössebageriet - Karlavägen 77
Tössebageriet is well known for its delicious cakes. They baked the royal wedding cakes for Crown Princess Viktoria's wedding and for her brother's wedding.

Petite France - John Ericssonsgatan 6
This is a bakery on Kungsholmen where you can eat a hearty breakfast or lunch, or just have some coffee with a delicious French pastry. They make fabulous cakes to order - the liquorice and *crème brûlée* ones are big favourites.

Vetekatten - Kungsgatan 55
This coffee and pastry shop has been here since 1928. Look out for rooms next to the entrance where you can sit peacefully and enjoy your cup of coffee.

Godis

The word for sweets or candies in Swedish is *godis*. When we wrote about Swedish food, we mentioned that Swedes have a taste for the strange combination of sweet and salty food. This may be the reason why they have a soft spot for liquorice and not just the normal liquorice you may be used to! It is extremely salty with an extra kick of ammonium chloride making it extra strong and salty on the tongue – delicious (or not)!

If you are adventurous enough to want try these liquorice sweets, they can be found in packets or loose (in pick & mix) in supermarkets. However if you can, do visit the speciality shop *Lakrits Roten* – there are five in Stockholm. The choice of liquorice products is large, ranging from toothpaste to liquorice crisps. They will happily show you their products and often have samples to try. An addictive experience!

Swedes consume a huge amount of *godis* (15 kilos/person/year) - a world record not to be proud of. The sale of *godis* peaks during the Christmas and Easter periods. At weekends you will see bags being filled at pick & mix stands in supermarkets when it is time for traditional *lördagsgodis* (Saturday sweet/candy time).

Stockholm Nightlife

The hub for the 'in crowd' is Stureplan in Östermalm, but there are plenty of other hot spots scattered around Stockholm. Around the Stureplan area you will find trendy bars such as Sturehof, Sturebaren, Tures, Grodan, Riche, Strandvägen 1 and Berns. At these bars young and old will gather for an 'AW' (ah-veh in Swedish), a term used to describe friends or colleagues getting together for a drink after work. During the summer season some bars also have outdoor areas.

Bars
In the summer. enjoy a sundowner and see Stockholm enveloped in rays of sun on the floating Strandbryggan or Ångbåtsbryggan on Strandvägen. Mälarpaviljongen on Kungsholmen is another floating bar for enjoying summer evenings and just opposite, on the island of Södermalm, there are fabulous views of Stockholm from Himlen, Mosebacketerrassen or Eriks Gondolen (opening 2022).

In the centre of Stockholm, near the train station on Vasagatan you can get a good view from the HIGH bar (Radisson Blu Royal Viking Hotel) or The Capital (Hotel Scandic Continental). When the weather is good, Strömterassen on the terrace of the Opera House has a fabulous view overlooking the Royal Palace. Round the corner is Operabaren – a relic from 1905, the interior reminiscent of an English private club. Nearby on Brunkebergstorg 4 is trendy TAK, an enormous roof-top area with an indoor restaurant where you can enjoy a Scandi-Japanese meal, a drink at the bar or take the sky walk over to their enormous open air roof top terrace (open during summer). As previously mentioned, Le Hibou at Bank Hotel has an outdoor terrace as well.

If you feel the need for a 'cool' drink then the Ice Bar is the place to go – an experience out of the ordinary where drinks are served in glasses made of ice and the interior of the bar carved entirely out of ice from the Torne river, in the north of Sweden.

Pubs

There are plenty of pubs in Stockholm and some are real classics. As its name implies, Zum Franziskaner is a traditional old German beer hall in Gamla Stan. Well-known pubs include Tudor Arms, Churchill Arms, Oliver Twist and the oldest Irish pub, The Auld Dub, just to mention a few. These can be good places for watching the rugby.

This section wouldn't be complete without mentioning the Vikings. If you want to soak up some of the atmosphere from the Viking era then Aifur in Gamla Stan is the place to go to taste some traditional mead – *Skål*!

By the way, take a short walk to the corner of Kåkbrinken-Prästgatan if you want to see a real Viking runestone dating from 1070-1100. It was used as part of the foundation when building the medieval cellar that still stands. Where it originally stood no-one knows. The inscription reads "Torsten and Frögunn erected this stone after…(illegible)….their son".

For the real beer enthusiast, why not join a Stockholm historic pub tour where you can taste your way through Swedish history from Viking mead to modern microbrews?
www.pubtour.se

Night Clubs

When it comes to clubbing in Stockholm, what's in and what's out can change overnight, so ask your trendy friends! Classic night clubs centrally located near Stureplan include Spybar, Sture Compagniet, Riche and Berns – last but not least the famous Café Opera. Fasching is a nightclub for jazz enthusiasts. By the water in Södermalm on Hornstullsstrand is Debaser, a large concert and club venue. Slakthuset is a club near Globen/Avicii Arena.

In the summer, legendary F12 Terrassen (Fredsgatan 12) opens up. Trädgården is another summer nightclub under Skanstull bridge, which moves indoors to Under Bron in the winter.

Health

Going to the doctor

In Sweden, you can register with a local doctor. You have the right to use the surgery or clinic of your choice when you need outpatient care. If it is not an emergency you should call 1177, ask for someone who speaks English (or your own language) and they will either give you advice online or refer you appropriately.

You can always call 1177 even just to ask about medication or simple medical questions – this can be especially helpful if you have children. They will provide advice and determine whether you might need to seek further care. Either call the number directly on your phone (this needs to be from a Swedish number) or consult their website (www.1177.se). At the bottom of their website page you can choose between 20 languages.

Normally a visit to a doctor/nurse will cost between 100-200 SEK each time. Specialist care may be more expensive. Once you have accrued costs exceeding SEK 1,200 within 12 months you are entitled to a *frikort* and you pay nothing more until the 12 months have passed.

Patients younger than 18 and older than 85 are free of charge unless they are hospitalised, then they pay SEK 100 per day for accommodation and food. A visit to A&E with your child costs SEK 120.

Contraceptives (*preventivmedel*) are either subsidised or free of charge up to the age of 25. A copper coil or IUD is free whatever your age. More information is available in Swedish on:

www.1177.se

Hair, Skin & Medical Conditions

The climate in Stockholm is incredibly dry and this may have an impact on health, skin and hair. Certain conditions which you may not have come across at home are commonplace in Sweden and it's as well to be aware of them.

Firstly, the dryness of the air, most particularly in the winter and when there is a lot of snow, can cause *krupp* ('false croup') chiefly in children. This can be very alarming, and you need to act quickly. Children may cough in a way that resembles a bark, is very dry sounding and insistent, usually owing to swelling in the upper respiratory tract. If mild, it can be helped by using a humidifier placed in the bedroom. However, if more acute, it can result in the child having difficulty breathing. It can help to take them into the bathroom with a hot shower running, producing lots of steam, or indeed exposing them to cold air. But if these acute symptoms are evident, it is best to go to childrens' A&E / the Emergency Room (*barnakuten*) at your nearest hospital (*sjukhus*), where treatment is quick and usually very effective in a short space of time.

Secondly, many expats notice a sharp increase in the number of nosebleeds experienced whilst living in Stockholm. This is probably also connected with the dryness of the air.

Less salubriously, Stockholm is also renowned for the 'winter vomiting bug' which does what you would expect. It tends to be fairly widely spread and you will probably feel very sick for a few days and then recover. Children have their fair share of this too and often bring it home from school.

Allergies can be a big issue in Sweden – with such a high ratio of forest this isn't very surprising, but birch allergies tend to be the most problematic. Sweden's national tree can cause havoc with some people experiencing strong allergic reactions when birch pollen levels are high, resulting in a very runny nose and itchy eyes. This can happen as early as January, months before leaves are on the trees. Symptoms may feel rather like hay fever but can become much more acute and affect breathing. If this is the case, a steroid injection is sometimes needed from the hospital. Immunotherapy treatment is also available if the allergy is persistent.

The Natural History Museum measures the pollen content in the air during spring and produces a daily report on *www.pollenraporten.se* or check *www.pollenkoll.se* which is also available as an app but here you need to use Google Translate.

Many of the weather forecast apps also report the pollen content in the air. To check your local weather the following websites and apps are useful:

www.yr.nu
www.smhi.se
www.klart.nu or *www.klart.se*

In terms of immunisation, as ticks are so prevalent in Stockholm's archipelago and forests, many people protect themselves with a course of injections against TBE (tick borne encephalitis). Information is available here and you should consult your doctor. For more information, consult *www.1177.se* - at the bottom of the home page, go to 'Other Language' choose 'English' and then in the search box enter 'Bitten by a tick'.

The fact that humidity is so low in the Stockholm area and that there is so little light during the winter months, means that you will need to look after your skin and hair. A good tip is to invest in a humidifier. There is a superb selection of skin products designed to help alleviate dry skin conditions, including:

24h repair cream from Acasia skincare. Smooth, rich and pleasant face cream that soothes and moisturises dry, chapped and red skin.

SOS rescue cream from pH formula. Soothing 24-hour cream that provides effective protection suitable for all skin types.

Emma S. product line by Swedish model Emma Wiklund. During winter, banish dry, dull skin and regain your radiance. Emma S treatment enzyme peel removes dead skin cells in just a minute.

Nimue Element barrier repair spf 20.
An additional moisturiser when it's cold outside, the best protection against moisture loss, cold and wind.

Lumene Harmonia nutri-recharging skin saviour balm.
Dense, oily balm that effectively treats chapped skin.

Ole Henriksen Nurture me moisturising cream.
Nourishing moisturiser with sunflower and rosehip oil, soothing allantoin and vitamin B5 which strengthens the skin barrier. Has an intense citrus scent.

The lack of light can impact your hair, resulting in modest or more noticeable hair loss. This can feel rather confusing and depressing, so it's reassuring to know what is causing it and there are also steps you can take to address it including a range of medication, such as Priorin, which can help rejuvenate hair. Consult your pharmacist for advice.

The lack of light can make many people feel very tired during the winter months, owing to depressed levels of vitamin D. It is common to take vitamin D supplements and again, consult your doctor or pharmacist for advice.

Something uplifting in the middle of the dark winter is a visit to the Edvard Anderson Conservatory at the Bergianska Botanic Garden (opposite the Natural History Museum), as this greenhouse has plants that need warmth and light, just like you! Or indulge in some light therapy in the public room at the back entrance of Centralbadet, a unique Jugend Palace with an Art Nouveau indoor pool in the centre of the city on Drottninggatan. There are other specialised places you can visit for some sun light therapy.
www.centralbadet.se

Driving & Parking

Driving in Sweden is a relief after many countries, as there is so much less traffic. However, you have to keep your wits about you as Sweden changed from driving on the left to driving on the right overnight one Sunday in 1967 and hence some older roads feel as if they are the wrong way round. Equally, you will spend much of the year driving in severe weather and need to be properly prepared.

Here are some key things to remember:

Speed limits
These are ferociously strict and you can expect to be stopped by the police and given a hefty fine if you are caught going above the limit, even by a very small margin. You will lose your licence if you drive 20km over the permitted 30km speed limit in a residential neighbourhood or school area. Be particularly observant on motorways, where speed limits can change with little warning on seemingly very empty sections of the road. Many of these roads also have speed cameras. You may feel as if you're the only person on the road and distances are often enormous, with signs indicating the speed limit occurring perhaps only every 7 kilometres, so it is easy to get caught out. If you are caught speeding, the police can take your licence away with only 24 hours' notice and this can be effective for 3 months. Check *www.trafikverket.se* for more information.

Drink driving
Drink driving rules in Sweden are similarly strict. Driving in Sweden while under the influence of alcohol, i.e. with a blood alcohol content of a minimum 0.02% or more, is regarded as a crime regardless of whether the driver is involved in an accident or not.

As a rule of thumb, half a glass of wine might be the maximum intake for an evening (this is the authors' experience, but we cannot vouch for others as each individual is different, depending on weight etc.).

Although it makes an evening out more expensive, it is very much worthwhile erring on the side of caution and using public transport and taxis, rather than running the risk of a drink driving offence.

Tomgångskörning (leaving your engine running) When you enter a residential area you are not allowed to leave your engine running for more than 1 minute, if you have pulled into the side of the road.

Parking
Parking is one of the most complicated challenges in Sweden, as there is a litany of very specific rules. Whilst it is always possible to ask a friendly Swede passing by or use designated car parks (*parkeringsplats*), it makes sense to be familiar with the following rules:

- You must always park with your car pointing the same way as the direction of the traffic on that side of the road
- Always check signs as you drive into the specific road on which you will be parking, as rules vary enormously. If there is a large white letter P on a dark blue background with arrows indicating where you are to park (and no other signs), you can park there.

- Residents Parking in Sweden is called *boendeparkering*. If you are resident in Stockholm and registered at the address that you are living at, you can contact *Boende Parkering* to find out if you are eligible for a parking pass. The price varies on where and when you are parking your car.
Tel. 08-508 263 00
Email: *boendep@stockholm.se*
- Special areas on the pavement are painted orange and these are loading areas with specific times - avoid them!
- Download the various parking apps – Easypark, Betala P, MobilPark, Aimo Park, P-Stockholm.
- You cannot park less than 10 metres/32.8 feet from crossings, corners, zebra crossings, bicycle lane intersections, pedestrian crossings, etc.
- Seatbelts must be worn at all times by front and rear-seat passengers when travelling in a car.
- Children who are less than 135 cm (4 ft 6 in) tall must use special safety devices when travelling in a car. These may be a baby seat, child seat, seatbelt seat or seat belt cushion, and must be adapted to the child's height. Never have them seated with the airbag function on.
- When driving in Sweden, your headlights must <u>always</u> be switched on, even in daytime.
- For more information *www.trafikverket.se*

Winter tyres
Winter tyres may be used between 1st October and 15th April if there are wintery conditions on the road i.e. covered in snow, icy or slippery and must be used between 1st December and 31st March in these conditions.
In the Stockholm area make sure that you change your tyres as soon as the frost starts setting in i.e. late October. All of a sudden there is a rush to change to winter tyres and you will be lucky to find a slot for tyre change at the garage. Don't leave it to the last moment!

Winter tyres may be studded (*dubbdäck*) or not studded (*friktionsdäck*). When buying new winter tyres, most people would probably recommend non-studded (*friktionsdäck*) as there are some restrictions for studded tyres, though they do ensure fantastic grip. It depends where you are likely to be driving most.

In some streets in Stockholm (as well as Gothenburg, Uppsala and Malmö), metal studded winter tyres are prohibited for environmental reasons (in 2020 this was the case in Hornsgatan, Fleminggatan and parts of Kungsgatan in Stockholm).

In very harsh winters, winter tyre dates may be extended into April. For more information check: *www.transportstyrelsen.se* go to the English page and search for congestion tax.

Winter tyres must have a minimum tread depth of 3 millimetres and summer tyres a minimum of 1.6 millimetres tread depth.

MOT (Ministry of Transport) or car inspection - *Bilprovning*
You will need to have your car checked annually. A reminder is normally sent out every year by post.
To find further information and to book, use this link: *www.bilprovning.se*. On their English page, go to *Boka Besiktning* on the left-hand menu and enter your car registration number. You can also call *0771-600 600*.

Car insurance and registration
If you are bringing a foreign car into Sweden, you have a certain time frame in which you must re-register it with Swedish number plates. You must also have valid car insurance. Consult here for more details:

www.transportstyrelsen.se
(in the search box enter import and choose relevant
information)

Importing a car from EU countries
- Clear the vehicle through the Swedish Customs
  Service (If you have imported the vehicle from a non-
  EU country)
- Pay VAT (If the vehicle is new and from another EU
  country.)
- Take out road traffic insurance for temporary
  registration with a Swedish insurance company
- Apply for verification of origin
- Make an appointment for a registration inspection
  and technical identity verification
- Test the roadworthiness of the vehicle.
- Allocate a registration number for your vehicle
- Activate your registration

If you are purchasing a new car, we would highly
recommend having an automatic heater for the engine and
car interior installed. This is incredibly useful in the winter,
meaning you can climb into a heated car and have good
visibility through the windows when the outside
temperature is below freezing. This can also be installed in
Sweden after purchase.

Stockholm congestion charge
A congestion charge is payable each time you enter
Stockholm. You will need to register your car for this, so
payments can be made by direct debit. Consult:
www.transportstyrelsen.se - go to the English page and
search for congestion tax.

Mobile phones
As of 1st February 2018, texting or fiddling with your phone
is not allowed. Keep your hands on the wheel!

Clothes Shopping

Shopping in Stockholm

City centres have an excellent choice of clothes shops, often also focused around sophisticated shopping centres or otherwise simply individual shops, boutiques or well-known brands – Scandinavian or international.

In Stockholm, head to Östermalm for high end shopping. The focal point is streets around Birger Jarlsgatan and Sturegallerian which has a stunning choice of fashion boutiques such as Louis Vuitton, Prada, Gucci etc. Another high-end small shopping centre is Mood on Mäster Samuelsgatan. The area between Birger Jarlsgatan and Hamngatan is full of excellent clothes shops and designer labels are to be found at the bottom of Birger Jarlsgatan. Sweden's iconic department store NK (Nordiska Kompaniet) is to be found halfway up Hamngatan. It is the oldest department store in Stockholm, built in 1915 by founder Joseph Sacks and designed by architect Ferdinand Broberg who was also the brain behind Thielska Gallery and Prince Eugen's Waldemarsudde. NK is worth visiting in December, as the windows are beautifully decorated with festive scenes, sometimes featuring star characters from the most  famous Swedish children's books, such as Pippi Longstocking and Findus the cat. Moving further towards T Centralen (the main railway station) and Regeringsgatan you will find more everyday shops with lower prices.

The longest pedestrian street – Drottninggatan - stretches all the way from Observatorielunden in Vasastan to Riksbron and the Swedish Parliament building near Gamla Stan (the Old Town) - the closer you get to Gamla Stan, the more souvenir and trinket shops appear. Back in the area around Östermalmstorg (underground station), the streets east of Birger Jarlsgatan have many unique shops running up as far as Karlavägen in some cases. Also, in the streets south of

Karlavägan in Östermalm there are a number of second-hand shops with clothes of amazing quality – really worth a snoop.

Gamla Stan, the medieval heart of old Stockholm is also dotted with different shops and weaving your way around the narrow streets is a fun way to spend a morning. You will find main street Västerlånggatan geared more towards tourists, whilst Österlånggatan features finer quality shops as well as quite a few renowned restaurants.

Södermalm is the largest of the 14 main islands of Stockholm and very popular amongst the young and hip! The area south of Folkungagatan called SoFo is full of interesting, trendy and contemporary shops specialising in clothing, design, jewellery, knickknacks, vintage, houseware, music and much more. Several fashion brands have their own stores in this district and you can find vintage shops here as well. With plenty of restaurants and cafés, the atmosphere is very laid-back. In summer, Nytorget Square is bustling – this is where you can visit many of the areas mentioned in 'The Girl with the Dragon Tattoo' and Stieg Larsson's other Millennium series books and which have featured in films. You can also go on a guided 'Millennium Tour'. From Södermalm there are some fabulous views of Stockholm - go to Fjällgatan and look out over the Baltic Sea with a view over to the islands of Gamla Stan, Skeppsholmen and Djurgården. If you want a great view over Lake Mälaren, climb up Skinnarviksberget (also a hangout for New Year's Eve) and look over to Kungsholmen and the Stockholm City Hall, then take a walk over to Monteliusvägen where you still can find some of the old red painted wooden houses that survived many of the Stockholm fires.

Shopping centres outside Stockholm
You will find lots of large-scale shopping centres with a vast range of shops and good parking facilities. These can be a particularly good option in winter, when their centrally heated car parks and the easy shopping experience can outshine struggling in cold, snowy streets. Around Stockholm these include:

- Täby Centrum
- Mörby Centrum
- Barkarby
- Kungens Kurva
- Kista Galleria
- Solna's Mall of Scandinavia (to be avoided on football match days when the Friends Arena fills up with fans)
- Nacka Forum
- Bromma Blocks (by Bromma Airport)
- In the centre of Stockholm, visit Mood, Sturegallerian and Gallerian, which also features an indoor skatepark

Shopping for the seasons – don't get caught out!

It is essential to plan for the season when buying clothes in Sweden. Supply is much more limited than in many other countries, so much as it's tempting to resist panic buying months ahead, you may be caught short on certain items if you don't buy in advance. This is particularly the case if you have children.

Realistically, in a normal winter you will be clothing them in ski suits every time you leave the house from November to March or April and it is entirely normal for these clothes to be worn to and from school and during every playtime. So, it makes sense to invest in really good kit and sturdy boots too.

For children, one of the best brands has always been Polarn O. Pyret – prices are quite high, but quality is superb and will stand you in very good stead for your winters in Sweden. XXL also has a very good range including footwear.

Department stores and supermarkets will also have ranges of winter clothing.

Swedes take appropriate dress very seriously, as the saying, *"there's no such thing as bad weather, only bad clothing"*, suggests. Children are also clothed in excellent waterproof clothing in autumn and spring which can also be sourced as above.

Online shopping
Amazon opened in Sweden in October 2020 and most other shops also have online shopping. They will either deliver to your home or to your nearest post office, which might be your nearest grocery shop or even the local newsagent/tobacconist.

Find out from your neighbours where the nearest pick-up point is located. Asking your neighbour or any local for information is the best way of getting to know a Swede - when they have a specific question to answer, they open up. Swedes are not famous for their small talk but are extremely happy to help if there is a specific problem that needs solving. This is key to approaching and getting to know your neighbours - maybe even use a question as an excuse to start up a conversation!

Sports Shopping

Incredible choice for all seasons

Sweden has an incredible choice of sports to try and a similarly amazing choice of equipment. The stand-out sports shop is XXL, a veritable emporium of every piece of sporting equipment you could possibly imagine, the entire product choice changing between summer and winter. You will find yourself walking through aisles of cross-country skis, ice fishing equipment and snow racer toboggans one moment, and cycling, kayaking and barbeque staples the next. See XXL's website and store-finder for stores around Stockholm. *www.xxl.se*

You may have heard of the classic and very popular *Kånken* backpack produced by Fjällräven - their shop is a haven for walkers, producing durable and high-quality gear. Other good sports shops include Naturkompaniet, Alewalds, Decathlon, Intersport and Löplabbet (especially if you need fitted sports shoes). Haglöfs, Fjällräven, and Didriksons are quite pricey but high-quality Swedish brands for outdoor activities. If you are looking for golfing gear, Dormy is the place to go or, in the city, Golf International on Holländargatan 6.

Second-hand sports equipment
Something slightly unexpected in an otherwise expensive country is
the fantastic range of second-hand sporting equipment available in
Sweden, which plays to the country's commitment to sustainability.
This makes it easy to buy skis, ski boots, skates, ice hockey equipment
and some sailing equipment at very reasonable prices. There are two
excellent shops towards Täby, about 20 minutes' drive north of
Stockholm:
www.sportbytarboden.se and *idrottonline.se/TabySLK-Skidor*

Both offer a fantastic range of second-hand skiing and skating
equipment. Other places for sourcing second-hand equipment and
clothes include:
www.secondhand.se
www.tradera.com
www.myrorna.se
www.blocket.se

Books

Books in Sweden are quite expensive. The main Swedish bookshop chains are Bokus, Adlibris, Akademibokhandeln and Pocketshop. The dedicated bookshop for English-language books and with an excellent range is The English Bookshop on Södermannag. 22 in Södermalm. If you are looking for childrens' books, Junibacken (the infamous and addictive children's museum) on Djurgården has a wonderful selection. Reading about Sweden, its history and enjoying its greatest authors will help give you a deeper insight into the country and its mindset.
www.bookshop.se

Reading Suggestions

The Saga of Gosta Berling - *Gösta Berling's Saga*
(by Nobel Prize winner Selma Lagerlöf)
A Swedish classic from 1891 – having been defrocked for misbehaving and drinking, priest Gösta Berling wants to die. The Mistress of Ekeby saves him from freezing to death and takes him in. As one of 12 party-loving homeless men in the manor at Ekeby, Gösta Berling becomes a leading spirit. But the evil Sintram lures the men into making a deal with the devil, which leads to the Mistress of Ekeby leaving home. Wild adventures, power struggles and redemption ensue.

Doctor Glas - *Doktor Glas*
(by Hjalmar Söderberg 1905)
Murder, suicide, euthanasia, abortion, women's rights... *Doctor Glas* was one of the most controversial books of its time. The story revolves around Doctor Glas who falls in love with his married patient. Having heard about her miserable sex life with her domineering clergyman husband, Doctor Glas eventually agrees to help her escape her unhappy marriage despite her having another lover.

He then agonises over whether to murder the husband and what the moral implications would be. At the time of publication, the book nearly ruined Söderberg's reputation, but today it's considered a classic.

City of my Dreams - *Mina Drömmars Stad*
(by Per Anders Fogelström 1960)
Per Anders Fogelström's series of five books chart the lives of Stockholmers between 1860 and 1968. During that time the city saw immense change and Fogelström's novels examine the very personal effect which events such as the introduction of the welfare system had on the lives of everyday people. The first four books are currently available in English and give you an insight into 'old Stockholm'.

The Emigrants - *Utvandrarna*
(by Vilhelm Moberg 1949)
The story of Kristina and Karl-Oskar, their friends, family and enemies, takes the reader through the crushing poverty that forced more than 1.5 million Swedes to emigrate to North America in the 1800s in search of a better life. The Emigrants' gripping tale is part history, part drama – and it will give you a deeper understanding of why Swedes have such a complicated relationship with both their own history and with America.

The Expedition - The Forgotten Story of a Polar Tragedy
(by Bea Uusma)
More than a century ago, three men set off on a hare-brained expedition to the North Pole – by air balloon. Decades later, their frozen bodies were discovered on a remote glacier, along with plenty of food supplies and warm clothing. This book by artist and doctor, Bea Uusma, sets out to discover what really happened to those men.

Astrid and Veronika
(by Linda Olsson)
A hauntingly beautiful account of a friendship struck up in a remote corner of Sweden between a young writer from New Zealand and an elderly lady who has led a reclusive existence for years, shunned by her village. A compelling and hugely touching story about how companionship and kindness allow a lady who embodies Swedish

self-sufficiency to open herself up to friendship and the outside world.

So Sweden – Living Differently
(by Alison Allfrey)
A journey from apprehension to almost unconditional adoration of a cool, distinct country, admired from afar, little known. Sweden. A rare expat's view of moving to a vast, detached, pristine country with a different DNA – the intrepid and enlightening story of a life-changing  posting to Stockholm of a family from a non-skiing nation.

The Almost Nearly Perfect People – Behind the Myth of the Scandinavian Utopia
(by Michael Booth)
A refreshing and objective assessment of what makes each of the Scandinavian countries tick, what lies behind Western Europe's fascination with the region and what each of these enigmatic and decidedly different countries thinks about its neighbours.

These books are available at The English Bookshop, on Amazon or you can buy a comprehensive set of Swedish classical authors from *www.novellix.se*

Swedish Crime

Swedish crime novels, or 'Scandi noir', became a genre of their own in the 1990s with the Wallander series by Henning Mankell. They have exerted a magnetic draw on readers across Europe with their plain language and eerie settings reeking of scope for the untoward to happen. They may not be what you want to read when actually living in Sweden, but if you're of a fearless disposition, read on! The following, which encompasses a classic murder mystery starring police inspector Kurt Wallander; a thrilling story by the author of the famous van Veeteren crime series; an action-filled page-turner by the man behind the bestselling Intercrime series and a nerve-racking tale from the deep, dark Swedish forests, would be a good first introduction.

www.novellix.se

You could also try:

The Girl with the Dragon Tattoo
(by Stieg Larsson)
The first of Stieg Larsson's Millennium trilogy, set on Södermalm, in Stockholm. They were made into films, first in Swedish and then in English with Daniel Craig as one of the actors. The book tells the story of two people attempting to investigate a billionaire with criminal links and has become a seminal work of 'Scandi noir'.

The Ice Princess, The Preacher, The Stonecutter
(by Camilla Läckberg)
A series of thrillers centred around the investigations of local detective, Patrik Hedström. Not for the faint-hearted, these bestsellers are driven by psychological intrigue and uncomfortable murders.

Swedish Classics

Here is an easy introduction to some of Sweden's most beloved authors translated into English.
www.novellix.se/eng.
It includes:

- Astrid Lindgren *Most Beloved Sister & Mirabelle*
- August Strindberg *Frictions* and *Miss Julie*
- Selma Lagerlöf *The Silver Mineland*
- Stig Dagerman *Sleet* and *A Moth to a Flame*

Swedish books for children

There are some wonderful treats for children, the themes of nature, carefree childhood and scheming pranks looming large, whilst there is also a wistful, timeless feel to these books, as well as a poignant awareness of what it is to be lonely or at the mercy of illness. Here are some favourite authors:

Astrid Lindgren
The Pippi Longstocking series, Emil series, Karlsson etc.

Sweden's most famous children's writer, who conjures up fantastical worlds and adventures through her vivid and mischievous characters – the rebellious Pippi Longstocking who lives with her favourite monkey and horse; Emil, the mischievous prankster farm boy from Småland; Karlsson the tubby man who flies over the roofs of Stockholm by pressing a button on his tummy......and others. Lindgren's works conjure up the wonderful innocence of Swedish country living for children, while also broaching her own grief at losing her son in some of her more sombre works, such as The Brothers Lionheart (recommended reading for adults).

Elsa Beskow
Peter in Blueberry Land, Children of the Forest, Pelle's New Suit, The Curious Fish – and more.

Elsa Beskow is sometimes referred to as the Beatrix Potter of Sweden and had illustrating and writing talents for small children to match. Living in Djursholm, just outside Stockholm, she centred her charming books around an idyll of Swedish country living in the 19th and 20th centuries, often with recourse to fairytale. These are stunning books with a timeless, innocent feel and well-suited to younger children.

Sven Nordqvist
The Pettson and Findus books

This is a completely irresistible series of books about a slightly

typical, lonely and grumpy old Swedish man looking for a companion in his isolation. This comes in the form of Findus, a chirpy, endlessly energetic kitten who arrives in a box of peas to change old man Pettson's life. The books follow his antics and adventures with gorgeous pictures and fast-paced writing, giving children a wonderful insight into Swedish rural life and some unforgettable characters, Pettson's hilarious collection of chickens first and foremost amongst these.

Tove Jansson
The Moomin books

Not Swedish, but Finnish, Tove Jansson was the goddess of magic for children having conjured up the wonderfully heart-warming and wholesome Moomins. This is a world of eccentric, brightly painted wooden houses, fishing trips, picnics, excursions into the forest, innocent flirtation by Moomintroll himself, all-encompassing motherly love embodied in the inimitable Moominmamma, carefree fatherhood à la Moominpappa, extraordinary creatures such as the silent Hattifatteners or the Hemulens who ensure order in the otherwise idyllic Moominvalley. A total breath of fresh air, these books will enchant and are available in formats for very young children, reading books for 7 to 10 year olds, not forgetting the legendary cartoons which will have adults or older children smiling for hours at their charm and pithy wit. You can see we're fans!

Films and series

A snapshot of unforgettable films and TV series which will give you a really Scandi feel:

The Cold Swedish Winter
A hilarious radio series starring many of Sweden's greatest comic actors and written by British comedian, Danny Robbins, this sitcom gives a pithy insight into what it's really like living in Sweden. It explores many of the country's more testing idiosyncrasies through Geoff who would do most things for his Swedish girlfriend, Linda, even if this involves eating moose, enduring endless snow, Swedish family dynamics and living in the cold and unpronounceable village of Yxsjö in northern Sweden. Available on BBC with a further series broadcast in December 2020.
www.bbc.co.uk

Welcome to Sweden
A very amusing sitcom written by American comedian Greg Poehler about his experiences moving to Sweden with his girlfriend, the stresses and strains of his 'new' Swedish family and the whole culture shock of this wonderful country with a mind of its own. The series was transmitted on NBC in the US without success, but Poehler's insights are wry and telling, and as a newcomer to Sweden you may well empathise with many of his impressions.
www.amazon.com and search for 'Welcome to Sweden'

A Man Called Ove
At once incredibly touching and darkly humorous, this film captures so perfectly the characteristics of many an elderly Swede – somewhat resigned to old age, emotionally introvert, used to struggling alone, unable or unwilling to seek help or company.............until some affectionate neighbours take him under their wing.
This is a really heart-warming film and gives such an insight into the compunction which drives Swedes to be self-sufficient and the relief they feel when offered the milk of human kindness. Also a book.

The Hundred Year Old Man who Climbed out of the Window and Disappeared

Another aged anti-hero who rebels against the confines of his old people's home and embarks upon a whole range of unlikely and increasingly incredible adventures. Somehow perhaps more for the male contingent, but amusing and thought-provoking – and also a book.

The Girl with the Dragon Tattoo

The film of the infamous Millennium series. There are two versions – the Swedish version filmed in 2009 and the English in 2011 starring Daniel Craig. Opinions differ as to which one is the best. Both were filmed in Sweden, primarily on Södermalm. Probably best not watched on your own and certainly not suitable for children.

Bron

Another Nordic noir crime television series where a corpse is found on the Öresund bridge connecting Denmark to Sweden. Police detective Saga Norén (who is believed to suffer from some type of autism) is faced with the challenge of solving the case together with her Danish counterparts.

Painters & Sculptors

Sweden has a number of artists whose renown may sometimes underplay their talent and are deserving of considerable appreciation. The country's phenomenal clarity of light, its unspoilt, vast landscape and abounding flora and fauna are often the subjects of these artists, who were sometimes also inspired by French schools of painting or indeed formed their own artist colonies. Stockholm has a wealth of excellent art galleries, listed later on.

In the centre of Stockholm, you can visit some of the major auction houses. Kaplans on Biblioteksgatan 5 have jewellery, watches and fashion paraphernalia such as vintage designer handbags, shoes etc. Bukowskis on Arsenalsgatan 2 is well worth a visit if only to have a look - it is a well renowned fine art and antique auction house established in 1870 and has simply stunning displays. Their English website is also excellent.
www.kaplans.se
www.bukowskis.com

Carl Larsson (1853-1919)
Larsson was a key exponent of Sweden's countryside idyll rendered in oils and watercolours. He was much influenced by the Arts & Crafts Movement whose romanticism and simplicity permeated his work. His beautifully decorated home, Lilla Hyttnäs, can be visited in Sundborn, Dalarna.

Anders Zorn (1860-1920)
Zorn was a master of sensual, almost tactile landscapes and portraits with a hint of Impressionism. He impressed kings and presidents alike, painting portraits of King Oscar II of Sweden, and American Presidents Cleveland and Roosevelt.

He was renowned for very restrained use of colour – 'The Zorn Palette' – often confined purely to yellow ochre, ivory black, vermilion and white. The place to appreciate his work is the National Museum of Fine Arts in Stockholm. The largest Zorn collection can be found in his hometown, Mora, at the Zorn museum.

Bruno Liljefors (1860-1939)
The most significant and influential wildlife painter of the late 19th and early 20th century in Sweden. His birds are particularly astonishing, combining as they do Impressionist brushstrokes and meticulous realistic observations. He had a vivid awareness of animals' anatomy and behaviour, having many in his garden at home, and his stunning painting 'Winter Hare' is one of his most famous and beguiling. There is a good collection of his work at the Thielska gallery.

Carl Wilhelmson (1866-1928)
Born in the fishing village of Fiskebäckskil, he is one Sweden's national painters and a depictor of the hard lives of fishermen. He also painted the landscapes of Uppland and Lapland, as well as a number of portraits.

Carl Eldh (1873-1954)
Carl Eldh was a contemporary of Carl Milles and one of Sweden's prominent sculptors. His home and studio were designed by his friend Ragnar Östberg, better known as the famous architect of the Stockholm City Hall. This unusual wooden building is now a museum and well worth a visit - just be sure to check their opening hours. From Carl Eldh's home in Bellevue Park which borders Vasastan there is a panoramic view of Brunnsviken and Haga - an unusually calm area in the middle of the city. Writer and friend August Strindberg was a frequent subject of Eldh's sculptures. The nude bronze sculptures 'The Song' and 'The Dance' in the park outside Stockholm's City Hall caused a bit of a stir amongst prudish Stockholmers when they were unveiled.

Carl Milles (1875 – 1955)
A master sculptor, significantly influenced by Rodin and Adolf von Hildebrand, he specialised in creating monumental fountains and fantastical figures, mixing the Classical and the Nordic through the juxtaposition of fauns, tritons and trolls. His own house and garden on Lidingö are sensational, with steep steps affording exquisite views across the water to Stockholm, whilst his rather surreal figures reach skywards from perilously high plinths. It's really something to behold, though the wind off the water is icy indeed in winter, so wrap up warm and abandon yourselves to the treats in store in the café afterwards.

John Bauer (1882-1918)
John Albert Bauer was a fabulous illustrator of landscape and mythology, but he also painted portraits. He is best known for his illustrations in *Bland tomtar och troll*, an anthology of Swedish folklore and fairy tales. Bauer's short career ended tragically when the boat he, his wife and son were travelling on capsized in a storm on Lake Vättern - they were on their way to start a new life in Stockholm. He was born and raised in Jönköping.

Art Galleries

Stockholm has an excellent choice of art galleries and the largest and most famous are listed below.

The National Museum
Newly renovated - a fabulous museum which needs to be visited quite a few times as it is very large. Don't miss the fabulous frescoes by Carl Larsson (1853-1919) on the main walls of the upper staircase. The large fresco depicting Gustav Vasa's entry into Stockholm and on the facing wall 'Midwinter Sacrifice' which was one of Carl Larsson's most controversial paintings. It is loosely based on the legend of King Domald from the *Ynglinga Saga*. His proposed sketch for this large painting was refused by the National Museum so he completed the project at his own expense, but again it failed to be accepted. In the 1980's it was sold at auction at Sotheby's in London and bought by a Japanese. Through donations it was eventually repurchased and long after Carl Larsson's death it finally found its rightful place in the entrance of the National Museum. You will see that it wouldn't fit anywhere else!

Fotografiska
Situated in Södermalm, this has a sensational view from its restaurant overlooking the water and Gamla Stan. An inspiring contemporary museum of photography. Under normal circumstances you can count on them always being open - every day 10 am to 11 pm! And the shop is fabulous for art books and imaginative presents too!

Artipelag
A spectacular, large privately owned gallery amongst the rocks and pine trees, on Värmdö in the archipelago, combining Art and Activities. In summer we recommend you take the boat (check *www.stromma.com*) to the art gallery and spend a day there. It boasts a great restaurant and lovely outdoor areas to walk around in.

You may have heard of the baby products from BabyBjorn, the most famous of which is the baby carrier - a baby-pack with your baby close in front, leaving your hands free. This was such a successful product enabling the founders to create this unique Art gallery. If you have taken the car to Artipelag you can easily extend your trip with a visit to Gustavsberg and the porcelain factory founded in 1825 which is nearby. Tableware with personalised décors is their speciality.

Waldemarsudde
Waldemarsudde was originally built as the private residence for Prince Eugene (1865-1947). He was himself an accomplished artist as well as an avid art collector having spent time studying art in Paris. Apart from his paintings which hang at Waldemarsudde, one of his most famous works of art is a 40m long mural that can be seen in the Prince's Gallery at the Stockholm City Hall, named after him. When he died, he bequeathed his home and collections to the Swedish state along with a donation to help cover the upkeep. The bequest included buildings, gardens, furniture, handicrafts and extensive collections of art.

He wanted it to be kept as if he still lived there, always with freshly picked flowers from his garden in the rooms. This is a truly gorgeous place to visit, with views over the water and particularly wonderful colours in autumn. There are permanent works and regular exhibitions – a really favoured spot in Stockholm and which can be reached by the number 7 tram from town. Don't forget to indulge at the Prince's Kitchen upstairs, where the soup, cakes and chocolate truffles are fabulous.

Liljevalchs
Under the authority of the City of Stockholm the Liljevalchs public art gallery opened in 1916 on the island of Djurgården, as the first

independent, public museum for contemporary art in Sweden. Each spring Liljevalchs opens its doors to a famous Spring Salon exhibiting contemporary art by unknown up-and-coming artists, where works are judged by a jury.

Thielska Galleriet

This museum is in a beautiful location on Blockhusudden on Djurgården. The house was created for the superb art collection of banker and art patron Ernest Thiel and was his home until 1924. The collection consists mostly of works from the turn of the 20th century by leading Scandinavian artists such as Carl Larsson, Edvard Munch, Eugène Jansson and Bruno Liljefors the renowned wildlife painter, who had an eye for capturing Swedish bird life and the amazing light of the archipelago and Swedish skies. The sculpture park contains works by Gustav Vigeland and Auguste Rodin. Don't miss the utterly gorgeous painting of an Arctic hare also by Bruno Liljefors.

Millesgården

Millesgården is an art museum and sculpture garden, located on the island of Lidingö. It is located on the grounds of the former home of sculptor Carl Milles and his wife, artist Olga Milles. Millesgården consists of three main parts: the artist's former home, an art gallery and a sculpture park.

There are also plenty of smaller and privately owned galleries scattered around on Södermalm, Vasastan, Norrmalm and Östermalm.

Swedish Design

Sweden is rightly famous for its amazing design ethic. There is something refreshingly simple and pure about this, in terms of an absolute dedication to optimising the use of light, focusing on clean lines and making things accessible. Nowhere is this more visible than in the case study of IKEA, founded by Ingvar Kamprad to distribute locally made furniture and subsequently championing the cause of affordable, stylish furniture with an eye to the future by selling it flat-packed. This howling success made him one of the richest men in the world, acting always, however, with great humility – perhaps an object lesson in Swedish reticence. IKEA now has more than 400 stores worldwide – and of course in Sweden!

At the other end of the scale, Svenskt Tenn (Strandvägen 5, Östermalm, Stockholm) is celebrated for its daring use of bright colour as a stand-out feature in what can be a very white decorative palate in Sweden. A producer of high quality pewter products at its origin, it quickly became synonymous with bold fabrics and prints by Josef Frank and first won international renown in Paris and New York from 1937. It is a mark of confident individual taste among design savvy Swedes to have a statement piece of Svenskt Tenn furniture (preferably by the classic renowned furniture designer Carl Malmsten) in a striking fabric as a contrast to otherwise serene pale shades. The shop is a true cornucopia of beautiful products, a feast for the eyes, and the café upstairs is a step into a bubble of sedate tranquillity and a huge treat.

Nordiska Galleriet on Nybrogatan 11 in Östermalm has a huge array of products from Scandinavia's top designers, as does Designtorget which has stores across Stockholm.

Klong is a very up-and-coming brand which is stocked in design shops across Stockholm and abroad, epitomising pared-back Scandinavian style. They also have a good webstore.

www.nordiskagalleriet.se
www.designtorget.se
www.klong.com

For more everyday needs – a hint of Swedish design, Christmas decorations, something for the kitchen – head to Åhléns, Sweden's largest department store which you will find everywhere and has a fantastic range of things synonymous with Swedish style at a reasonable price.

Working in Sweden

The working environment in Sweden may be very different to what you are used to. It has pluses and minuses.

On the positive side, management structures are extremely flat and there is very little hierarchy, so you can expect your voice to be heard and for you to be consulted about decisions in a consensus fashion. Swedes are also very realistic and accepting about the fact that many people have children and a family life, so this makes for much more flexible working hours than in some other European countries.

Expats are often surprised that Swedish colleagues arrive in the office later than them and leave earlier, and this means that staff car parks often empty from the back (those who arrive last also leave first!). So it is not an issue if you need to pick children up from school or want to finish your work later in the evening, once family activities and supper have been accomplished.

When introducing yourself to colleagues, it is perfectly normal to mention your children first, rather than how many years you have worked in your sector, for example – there is no façade when it comes to work and family co-existing. As a mirror reflection of very high levels of equality between the sexes in Sweden, you are likely to find a very even split of men and women in the workplace, even in areas such as technology and engineering which can be skewed in one direction in other countries.

On the more challenging side of the equation, the determination to hear all voices and achieve consensus decisions can lead to many long hours of meetings every day, making it difficult to get 'work' done. Motivating and managing teams is also a very different prospect and may take patience and lateral thinking.

Furthermore, as Swedes tend to shy away from open conflict if there is an issue with a colleague, you are more likely to hear about it by email than in a meeting. This scope for being 'passive – aggressive' can leave you feeling baffled and is another challenge in developing good working relationships with colleagues.

Lastly, Swedes tend not to expect to socialise with colleagues and companies employing expats seem to make little effort to help people forge a social life. All the more reason to find activities and clubs in keeping with your interests, which will give you the opportunity to meet people in other ways. The exception to this rule can be company Christmas parties which sometimes involve saunas – the etiquette for this can be a surprise to newcomers, so be prepared!

Some other dynamics of working in Sweden are very particularly Swedish. There is considerable prestige and pride attached to working for one of Sweden's 'national champions' – its largest, most longstanding companies. Hence people who have dedicated more than 25 years of service to their company will attend a special presentation and ceremony to celebrate this.

Whilst English is spoken to a very high level in very many companies, it pays to remember that you are working in Sweden and that if you learn some Swedish, it will act as a mark of respect and help bring you closer to colleagues, as well as getting on the 'inside track'. Sometimes the really crucial conversations are held only in Swedish, which is understandable.

Some people, if not on an official work posting, manage to bring their freelance work with them and this is what Alison did. This work provided a welcome structure to her life and extra fulfilment. It wasn't without its complications, though, as many an hour on the phone to the Swedish tax office confirmed. It is advisable to take your time with this too, expect lots of complicated forms relating to tax and child benefits – and hope that you have neighbours as patient as she did to help decipher the forms. It is also a very good idea indeed to use a Swedish accountant to help you with your tax return.

You may find that living abroad presents lots of opportunities to be entrepreneurial and try something you've never ventured into before. People from different countries often import special products from their country and sell them from their homes. Or you may find yourself setting up a children's singing group or learning to teach yoga. Sometimes things just don't quite exist as you would like them, so there are exciting opportunities to create them.

There are some companies offering post-relocation services such as assisting in job searches for spouses. Grow International is one of these. You can also check out New To Sweden as well as Undutchables. There are other employments agencies to be found on the internet as well as the Swedish Public Employment Agency's (*Arbetsförmedlingen*) who offers support to people looking for work in Sweden.

www.newtosweden.org
www.undutchables.se

Getting Outside

Few countries are more geared towards the great outdoors than Sweden. Levels of exercise-taking are really striking and almost whatever the weather, people are outside and active. Opportunities vary enormously according to the season, but there is a welter of possibility at your fingertips.

Running and walking
In such a vast country, opportunities for running and walking are endless. The two most obvious settings are by the water or in the forest and both are uplifting.

In and around Stockholm, some of the loveliest places are in the grounds of Ulriksdals Slott on the banks of Edsviken (lake) which itself has several miles of footpath along its shores and wonderful views. The Royal Parks offer wonderful opportunities and Hagaparken is another favourite - it also has a stunning butterfly house which is a good complement to a winter walk. It is stiflingly hot inside, so you will find yourself carrying your winter clothes. In the autumn, Tyresta National Park in the Tyresö region has particularly amazing autumn colour as do the gardens of the Waldemarsudde gallery on Djurgården in Stockholm.

Ulriksdals Slott - www.kungligaslotten.se (look under Royal palaces)
Hagaparken - www.visithaga.se
Waldemarsudde - www.waldemarsudde.se

When walking, it's important to be aware of the concept of *allemansrätten* – this allows everyone the right and freedom to access the countryside. You can roam freely and explore nature without having to wonder if you are trespassing or not (private gardens exempt). You are also permitted to pitch a tent temporarily as long as you do not disturb, harm, litter or damage wildlife or crops. You can also make a campfire with proper safety precautions but need to be aware of local fire guidelines and regulations. You may

99

also enjoy the spoils of nature, pick berries and mushrooms, and also fish with a rod in still waters. If this appeals to you then be sure to include a hike in the north of Sweden on your to do list - preferably during summer or early autumn.

The most famous and classic route is *Kungsleden*, the King's trail, a 400km long trail between Abisko and Hemavan. You can join the Swedish Tourist Association who provide a wealth of information about hikes and trails and also offer reduced prices for accommodation if you are not lugging your tent along with you.

www.swedishtouristassociation.com

If running is your thing, then you will be in good company with the myriad of Swedes who run diligently every weekend and also in the evening. This website offers lots of good suggestions for running trails around Stockholm: *www.komoot.com*

Djurgården is a serene and tranquil oasis in the middle of Stockholm. It becomes a bit more of a *lemmeltåg* (exodus) at the weekend when every Stockholmer is out stretching their legs. The island itself is part of the world's first national urban parks and forms a green lung more than 6 miles long - from Djurgården in the south to Sörentorp and Ulriksdal in the north. It contains many of the city's most famous museums and cultural attractions (the *Vasa* Museum, *Gröna Lund*, the ABBA museum and *Skansen* to name a few) with green nature, parks, and family-friendly activities. Djurgården can be reached by bus, tram or ferry from central Stockholm. A walk along fashionable Strandvägen, from The Royal Dramatic Theatre to Djurgårdsbron, is highly recommended. To see what is happening on Djurgården this is their website: *www.royaldjurgarden.se*

For further inspiration, consult *www.calazo.se* which has a wealth of tips and suggestions for walking and biking trails or *www.visitstockholm.com*

There are many walking and running groups to be found on the internet and Facebook and this is a great way to meet new people

Cycling
Sweden is paradise for cyclists, with endless dedicated cycleways. It becomes a way of life and is a particular joy in the summer, when the evenings seem endless and the air fragrant with the scent of flowers in abundance. Cycling is also an excellent way to enjoy views over the water. Weekends see Djurgården in Stockholm full of cyclists (in an uncluttered Swedish way), particularly along the sides of the beautiful canal which leads out towards the open water.

In winter it takes on a different complexion and for the really intrepid, you can buy studded cycle tyres from XXL and other sports shops. Conditions can be very slippery indeed, so be extremely careful.

The County Administrative Board of Stockholm has signposted a 36 km (22 mile) bike route from Ulriksdal to Blockhusudden. You can download a map of the route from their website: *www.nationalstadsparken.se*. Further suggestions for cycle rides around Stockholm are available here: *www.komoot.com*

The city is promoting the use of bicycles as a mode of transport. To help commuters, they have produced a city map showing all bicycle lanes which you can check out on their website: *cykla.stockholm/cykelnat*

You may notice that most bikers wear helmets - this is mandatory for children. If you find the helmet a bit offputting and not the most exciting fashion accessory, a new Swedish invention is the *Hövding* - an airbag to protect your head, which means you can cycle in elegance! *www.hovding.com*.

Tennis

With Björn Borg and Stefan Edberg as the fathers of Swedish tennis, the country has a strong track record in the sport and you will find a good number of tennis clubs available. In Stockholm itself, try Kungliga Tennishallen or Stadion, whilst to the north of Stockholm there are excellent clubs in Djursholm, Danderyd and Näsby Park, all of which are perfect places to meet both Swedes and other expats. You will need to be organised and book courts quite far in advance as they are very popular. Lessons are available for both children and adults, and there are drop-in sessions for adults in the mornings at Danderyd. Courts are mostly indoor, but there are some outdoor ones too including Hagatennis situated in the grounds of Hagaparken and open from April to October.

If you have the opportunity, going to the Nordea Swedish Open Tennis tournament in Båstad is a wonderful experience. The courts are set right next to endless sandy beaches, the village itself is idyllic with small wooden houses covered in climbing roses. It's a great excuse to discover some of the south-west coast of Sweden and all very laid back and fun.

www.dtk.se (Danderyd)
www.djtk.se (Djursholm)
www.nptk.se (Näsby Park)
www.hagatennis.se
www.nordeaopen.se

Golf

Despite the weather, golf has become something of a national sport with nearly 500 golf clubs from north to south producing some world-renowned Swedish golfers such as Jesper Parnevik, Annika Sörenstam and Henrik Stenson. Many of these golf courses are used for cross country skiing in winter.

Near Stockholm there is a golf course on Lidingö, a short-hole course Ekholmsnäs Golf, as well as courses at Djursholms Golfklubb,

Danderyd, Stockholms Golfklubb and Ulriksdal.
www.lidingogk.se
www.ekholmsnasgolf.se
www.dgk.nu
www.danderydsgk.se
www.stockholmsgolfklubb.se
www.ulriksdalsgk.se

The season will be longer in the south, but during summer you can play all day and night under the midnight sun! To find a golf course near you go to: *www.1golf.eu*

Gyms
There is a good range of gyms in Stockholm. The main chain with plenty of sites around the city is SATS. Friskis & Svettis offers work-out classes, while Becore focuses more on full body workout sessions as well as cycling. Other options are Djursholms Träningscenter in Djursholm, Miramadi on Lidingö as well as Nordic Wellness with 267 gyms around Sweden.
www.sats.se
www.friskissvettis.se
www.becore.se
www.dtc.se
www.miramadi.se
www.nordicwellness.se

Yoga
In Stockholm itself, Yogayama is Scandinavia's leading yoga operation and has sites in Östermalm and Sjöstaden offering a whole variety of classes and types of yoga, for adults and children alike. It also provides English speaking teachers.
www.yogayama.com

If you're looking for a fantastic yoga experience just outside Stockholm, Djursholm Yoga usually offers 16 classes a week, catering from children to older people and everyone in between and covering Vinyasa, Hatha, Yin and Ashtanga yoga. The studio is small and cosy,

with classes conducted in English if required. Owing to the current Covid situation they also offer outdoor classes on a Stocksund rooftop terrace with views over the forest! The atmosphere is very personal and friendly.
www.djursholmyoga.se

Pilates
Try Pilates FleuriForm in Djursholm, run by Yasmin Nordmark where you can take part in a class or have personal tuition. Yasmin also caters for older people, children and men.
Contact: *Yasmin.nordmark@icloud.com*

Other Pilates classes can be found on the following site: *www.pilates-center.se*

Padel
The latest trend in Stockholm is padel - courts are popping up everywhere. Padel is typically played in doubles on an enclosed court, smaller than a standard tennis court. The balls used are similar to tennis balls and are allowed to bounce off the surrounding walls, but the rackets are different. You can locate the closest court to you on the following website:

www.padelcup.se then click on *padelbanor*.

Indoor Swimming Pools
Sturebadet is centrally located in Sturegallerian on Stureplan, and is a beautiful exclusive spa with group training classes in two fitness studios, one for cardio and strength training and another for body and mind, as well as.an indoor pool. You can also visit it just to eat a healthy lunch while watching the swimmers from your table from the gallery above.

Centralbadet is another indoor pool on Drottninggatan 88, right in the heart of Stockholm. At the historic Art Nouveau style Centralbadet dating from 1904 you can swim in a 25 metre pool, book a massage or relax in their unique Nordic sauna. On site you will also find a restaurant, a well-equipped gym, yoga, light therapy, a classic barber shop and an outdoor terrace with a vintage gym.

Check your local area to find your nearest indoor pool. There are plenty in and around the Stockholm area.

Riding

Riding is a massively popular sport in Sweden, second only to football! You will see horses everywhere and Sweden competes at very high levels in international competitions for both show-jumping and eventing - as mentioned elsewhere, the Swedish International Horse Show is a fantastic display of equine talent. If you want to ride, try Djursholm's Riddklubb which is one of the largest riding schools in the country. The school offers lessons, competitions and holiday courses and you can choose between a fantastic range of both horses and ponies.

www.djursholms-ridklubb.com

In the city there is Swartlings Ridskola as well as Djurgårdens Ridskola and if you venture out to Lidingö there is Stockby Ridskola. You will also find pony riding at Lidingö Ponny Ridskola at Elfvik farm.

www.swartlingsridskola.se
www.djrk.se
www.ridskolanstockby.se
www.lidingoponnyridskola.se

You can also enjoy the unique seasonal experience of an early morning tour on horseback through Stockholm, before the city wakes up. They also arrange tours on the riding paths of centrally located Djurgården and the Liljanskogen forest.

www2.stockholmbyhorse.se

Summer Swimming

Water is ever present in Sweden and you will often feel the urge to get in! The best opportunities are of course in the archipelago with its more than 25,000 islands providing unending secluded spots for a dip.

Lake Mälaren also offers endless places. Your nearest beach on Mälaren is on Långholmen near Södermalm or by Rålambshovsparken on Kungsholmen. If you live in the centre of Stockholm, you will find Erikdalsbadet and Kampementsbadet, two centrally located open air pools/lidos.

To find your closest outdoor pool consult:
motionera.stockholm/hitta-utomhusbassang/

There is also Breviksbadet, a large outdoor pool area on the island of Lidingö.

Winter Swimming
In the winter, swimming is an entirely different proposition, involving a sequence of warming up in a sauna before taking the plunge into icy water and retreating to your wooden cabin to warm up again. During the Corona pandemic, winter swimming without the warmth of a bastu reached an all-time high. Places where you can try this include:

Hellasgården in Nacka:
hellasgarden.se

Tanto Bastu at Tantolunden Hornstull/Södermalm:
tantobastuforening.se

Saltsjöbadens Friluftsbad in Saltsjöbaden:
saltisbadet.se

Many hotels offer packages where the sauna is included. If you want to discover the archipelago during the winter months, then don't miss a visit to the island of Smådalarö. This is a 45 minute drive south of Stockholm and you can book your own sauna at Hotel Smådalarögård. Or you could have a go closer to Stockholm, at Vår Gård, Saltsjöbaden or Ellery Beach House on Lidingö. For more information, consult:
www.smadalarogard.se

www.vargard.se
www.ellerybeachhouse.com

Bastu - Sauna
Otherwise, why not do something out of the ordinary and book a unique sauna on Strandvägen, right in the middle of Stockholm, at *www.glashuset.com*

Some saunas are mixed gender and in public places you will go in with a towel on (you can be naked underneath or not) - if there are other people there you can choose to stay wrapped up. This may vary depending on where you are, and you just have to follow what everyone else does. However, if you are invited to take a sauna in someone's private home don't be offended if they are naked - you can still stay wrapped up and nobody will be offended! Always shower before entering the sauna and, needless to say, afterwards too. Bring a towel to sit on and one to dry yourself with (and one to wrap around you)!

Don't miss out on the fabulous sauna experience.

Why not try one in winter with a dip in an *isvak* - which is basically a large hole in the ice on a frozen lake or sea!

Getting Around on the Water

Water is omnipresent in Sweden and plays tricks with where you think places are. Often you can drive miles in a car to make a journey which would be so much more direct by boat. Not to mention the fact that being on the water is the most elemental, stunning and revealing way to discover the landscape around Stockholm. Blessed with an archipelago of more than 25,000 islands the scope for exploring is endless. This is the best way to soak up the atmosphere of the myriad tiny and larger islands with their granite rocks shelving into the water, their opportunities for fishing, the gentle lapping of the brackish (only slightly salty) water and the sense of having left the busy world behind you.

Ferries
There is a fantastic system of ferries, leaving either from central Stockholm or from Vaxholm. The main decision is whether to go west into Lake Mälaren or east into the archipelago. You can also visit the King's summer palace, Drottningholm, by boat.

To reach these destinations you can choose one of Strömma's numerous tours. They usually depart from 3 main ports in the city which are: Nybroviken on Strandvägen, Strömkajen close to the Grand Hotel and if you are travelling on the lake it departs from Klara Mälarstrand just opposite Stockholm City Hall. They have numerous seasonal guided tours, day trips and fabulous dining cruises.
www.stromma.com

Otherwise you can use Vaxholmsbolaget, owned by Stockholm county council which is responsible for seaborne public transport in the Stockholm archipelago and Stockholm harbour.
www.vaxholmsbolaget.se

Here are some direct links to websites for some of the main islands in the Stockholm archipelago:
www.grinda.se
www.uto.se

www.visitsandhamn.se
www.fjäderholmarna.se

The quickest and closest place for your first taste of the archipelago is Fjäderholmarna, no more than 20 minutes from Stockholm (from Strandvägen or Slussen) and which encapsulates the characteristics of the islands – lots of fresh fish, glassblowing to watch, artists' studios and an array of good restaurants and cafés. This is the archipelago in a snapshot. Or you could visit Artipelag on Värmdö, where you can soak up the most ravishing spot for an art gallery surrounded by the archipelago and be revived by cutting edge exhibitions and excellent food.

However, for those who have time to soak up the archipelago at a slower pace and really get away from it all, don't miss the opportunity to venture further. Vaxholm itself is very small, but has some excellent clothes, lifestyle and sailing shops and serves as the perfect gateway to the treasures of the archipelago. Stop, too, for delicious cakes and sandwiches either near the water, or a few minutes outside at Café Parkvillan near Bogesunds Slott. Hopefully by the summer of 2021 the Vaxholm Hembygdsgårdens summer café will have opened again after a fire – indulge in their famous *smörgåsbord* of cakes and pastries and enjoy these with a strong cup of coffee in their garden by the water's edge. If you're in your own boat, Vaxholm is the place to fill up with fuel and if you've driven there, you will find a vast choice of islands to visit by ferry.

As you leave Vaxholm, you wind your way past the fort in the water and through a narrow channel passing the first picture postcard archipelago houses in soft pastel tones or Sweden's signature deep terracotta red. Then the water opens out and the archipelago stretches before you.

If you're looking for an overnight stay, then Grinda *(www.Grinda.se)* is a good spot, with *stuga* (wooden cabins) for rent and lots to do *(www.skargardsstugor.se).* You can walk through lovely meadows, picnic, swim from the beaches or eat in first rate restaurants. And every time you glimpse the water, there will be an elegant sailing boat or two bobbing gently in the water, summing up understated Swedish style as the water glimmers behind it.

Another personal favourite is Finnhamn, with memories of fishing for perch (*aborre*) from warm rocks. Or Gällnö – take a boat from Strömkajen in Stockholm or by the Grand Hotel and wonder at this fabulous island which really gives you a chance to spread your wings. This is the island for those who want to walk, picnic and explore. There is even a rowing boat provided by the local council at the end of one footpath which you can use to row yourselves over to the adjacent island. It has trees and meadows aplenty and is a veritable haven of space and tranquillity.

Private Boat/Rentals
Of course, the most independent and liberating way to see the archipelago is with your own boat. This needs some planning but is hugely worthwhile. If you are living in Sweden for some time, it may be worthwhile – but expensive – to buy one. Think carefully about this – as the old saying goes, "the two best days of owning a boat are the day you buy it, and the day you sell it!". Otherwise, you can either rent one for the summer season or a shorter period of time or join a 'sharing club'. Renting a boat for a weekend, week or few weeks is

relatively much more expensive than renting one for a longer period of time so beware.

The key challenge is where to moor your boat, as places in marinas are very difficult to come by, but you may find a friend with a mooring which comes with their waterfront house, or you may be able to borrow someone's for a season.

The best option for renting a boat is through Blocket, Sweden's own answer to Ebay.

Go to *www.blocket.se* and search under *Annonser*. Enter '*motorbåt*' for motorboat or '*segelbåt*' for sailing boat. Where it says *Typ av annons* either click on *Köpes* (if you want to buy) or *Uthyres* (if you want to rent).

Ideally rent for the whole season to bring the cost down, or you could also consider doing this excluding July which is when all the Swedes take their holidays and by giving the boat back for this month, when you may be away anyway, the expense will be less. In any case, start your research really early to avoid disappointment – ideally the previous September.

If you feel more comfortable with sharing, try:
agapiboating.com

In terms of what to rent, this will be conditioned by budget and availability, but a priority might be to have a boat with a cabin – this is great for wetter moments, as well as providing somewhere for younger children to play or rest.

Before setting out, you will need to buy sailing charts. Try Captains on Kommendörsgatan 26 in Stockholm or online at *www.nautiska.se/sjokort*. If you're based around Djursholm or Täby, then the expanse of water between them and Vaxholm will be your first playground. This includes Stora Värtan and there is an idyllic lake called Kyrkfjärden which is accessed by a very narrow opening which will require some careful navigation. Once you've built your confidence to go beyond Vaxholm, do try Grinda, Finnhamn or Gällno which are within fairly easy reach. There you can find somewhere to camp.

In terms of navigation, remember never to aim for a seagull – they tend to be sitting on a rock!

You don't officially need particular training in driving a boat in order to rent one, but it's obviously useful.

Check out *www.skipperi.com* where you can choose from a fleet of privately owned boats in different harbours within Stockholm. Another option is their own fleet of boats which you can subscribe to and use whenever you choose, through their booking system - here you might need some help with the language as the website is not yet in English.
www.skipperi.se

Other boat rental services:
www.agapiboating.se
www.clickandboat.com
www.nautal.com

Fishing
Fishing is a year-round pastime in Sweden. In winter, you will see people patiently crouched over a small hole in the ice, dug with a corkscrew shaped tool. The main prizes are pike, zander and perch. You can buy the right equipment at XXL and will need huge amounts of warm clothing and patience. Or visit Lundgrens fish and tackle shop on Storkyrkobrinken 12, a fisherman's haven that has been in the Old Town since 1892.

Fishing is altogether more relaxed in the summer, where you can sit on a warm rock in the archipelago sun and tease a perch out of the water, before cooking it for supper. Life's simple pleasures! You will also see people fishing near Parliament in the centre of Stockholm. All Swedes are permitted to do this thanks to a decree made by Queen Christina in 1636.

Winter Sports

Skating

The summer is over, the boat is gone from the mooring, snow is on the ground, but crucially has Norrviken frozen yet?

Nordic skating in Stockholm is second only to boating in the archipelago, but luckily you don't have to choose between them as they have their own distinct seasons. It is challenging, exhilarating and requires a good dose of bravery and fitness, but that said, many Swedish families will push Granny on the ice in a specially adapted chair with skate attachments, *'spark'*, whilst babies nestled in sheepskin rugs are often to be seen whizzing around in their prams, pushed by ultra-fit parents. It's a fantastic opportunity for people watching.

The first step is to find a friendly Swede who can tell you how it all works, where to go, what the ice conditions are. The second is to head to XXL or another sports shop to invest in special walking boots to which you attach long skating blades – forget your figure skates, as they will wobble horribly on the natural ice. You will also want skating poles to help propel yourself forwards and which help with balance, as well as testing the sturdiness of the ice. Lastly, be sure to wear a helmet for the obvious reason that the ice is unforgiving and extremely hard.

On the ice always wear ice claws around your neck which will act as a grip to pull yourself out of the ice, should you fall through. Also, if you are taking this seriously or going far, rule number one is never to venture out on the ice alone. Bring along a safety rope, a backpack with a change of clothes wrapped in a plastic bag. You also need to check the ice conditions to find out which areas are safe on the day you want to skate.

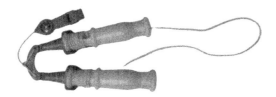

Consult *www.sssk.se* the website of *Stockholms Skridskoseglarklubb* (skating club) which also organises skating outings or *motionera.stockholm/sjoisbanor.*

Ice conditions vary hugely – the most sought after is when new rain has frozen, making for mirror-like ice which is incredibly smooth and gives off the most stunning reflections of the sky and clouds. Ice which has thawed and refrozen many times is much bumpier and some skateable ice may have a couple of inches of water on which can feel off-putting. Be warned that, unless you go out with a guide who will have made an assessment, you need to make decisions about safety yourself as the Swedish attitude is that you need to look after yourself rather than relying on 'health and safety' protocols.

You can then head to a number of lakes around Stockholm which are hotspots (or rather absolutely freezing) for skating. These include:

- Norrviken (offers equipment for hire)
- Edsviken
- Garnsviken, Brottby
- Vallentunasjön

Don't forget to bring a rucksack with plenty of hot chocolate and *pepparkakor* to keep you warm.

For the more confident or intrepid, you can take your new skating legs to further lengths by touring around other lakes and even parts of the archipelago in really cold winters with a guide. Contacting *www.stockholmadventures.com* is a good place to start for some incredible experiences.

There are also a number of skating races across Sweden for a further rush of adrenalin, the *Vikingarännet* being the most famous, as well as one which starts from Sigtuna. There are more races further north and west of Stockholm – ask the specialists.

This is an amazing experience which can form a key part of your winter weekends. And it's also an excuse to learn another wonderfully complicated Swedish word – *skridskoåkning*.

Skiing
The beauty of skiing in Sweden is that it's a very natural, relaxed, family-oriented activity. Although people do go to Åre in the north (approx. 6 hours' drive from Stockholm) for set piece holidays, much skiing activity takes place just at weekends by throwing the kit in the car and going to places anywhere between 10 minutes and 2-3 hours from Stockholm.

The very closest you will get is the artificial slope at Hammarbybacken, a matter of minutes from the city centre and with four short slopes, or Ekholmnäsbacken which provides easy slopes for children and newcomers to the slopes on Lidingö. The highest slopes local to Stockholm can be found at Flottsbro, whilst Ekebyhovsbacken has a ski school, as well as floodlit slopes. Ragnhildsborgsbacken is close to Södertälje and focuses mostly on children and affordable skiing.

Further afield, Romme Alpin in the Dalarna region and 2 ½ hours from Stockholm is a fully fledged ski resort with 30 slopes, complete with a ski-in hotel. Further afield still, Kungsberget is 220km north of Stockholm, or Sälen is 5 hours away near the Norwegian border and offers 100 slopes in 4 different areas. Another option is Bjursås.
www.rommealpin.se
www.kungsberget.se
www.bjursas.com

The pace of skiing and these resorts is much quieter than what you may have experienced in the Alps or elsewhere. It is very laid back, charming and well-suited to children finding their feet on skis whilst also providing enough challenges for more competent skiers. Expect an unpretentious, family-centric experience with parents mostly teaching their own children, except for in larger resorts where ski school is available (*www.skistar.com* offers lessons in a number of these).

The very skilled will want to make the journey to Åre for a really full range of slopes. The emphasis is also on affordability and low-key family fun, so expect welcoming mountain cafes with pancakes, goulash soup and hot chocolate aplenty, as well as lots of chalets on the slopes reserved for families wanting to eat picnics or cook sausages. At Easter, the Easter witch may also visit the slopes in full dress, offering sweets to children.

Cross-country skiing
This is one of the main delights of the Swedish winter and a wonderful way to get real enjoyment out of the snow. It is not rare to see people with cross-country skis slung over the shoulder right in the middle of Stockholm in a good winter and there is seemingly no age limit for skiers, with octagenarians frequently likely to outpace people decades younger through sheer hard-won expertise and endurance.

It is not a difficult sport to embark upon and much less frightening than pointing your skis downhill, but it is very much worthwhile getting some instruction from a Swede or Norwegian if possible, as good technique makes all the difference in terms of how far you get and how you can maximise the return on effort expended. The secret is to make your body work in diagonals, with opposite arms and legs moving forward together to propel you forward. If you can achieve a real glide with this, then you will surge forward in the track – avoid the obvious beginners' style of simply wiggling rather rigid hips / bottom.

Remember that ski tracks are beautifully prepared into thick, crisp furrows and Swedes will very much frown upon anyone who cuts across the tracks with their skis. So, if you are feeling a little out of control on the more downhill sections (the skis are very light, after all), simply lift your right ski and put it in the left hand track, moving your left ski outside the left track. That way you can snow plough with the left ski (while nobody is looking), which will act as an effective braking system whilst not destroying the tracks. Creating V shaped sections across the tracks is totally permissible when going uphill, which necessitates putting your skis together in said V and waddling upwards with each ski cutting slightly into the snow to avoid you sliding backwards, to gain some traction. This part can be fairly exhausting and makes you look like a cross between a duck and a penguin.

In terms of equipment, you will need cross-country skis and specific boots which clip onto them and are rather like walking boots, as well as poles. As you get very hot, go against your instincts and shed your really warm winter coat for something lighter. If you have small children, you can sometimes hire or could invest in (though expensive) a very specialised toboggan which you can pull behind you.

You will find cross-country ski tracks open up everywhere, including at golf clubs such as Djursholm, Lidingö and Danderyd. In Stockholm there is a track on Gärdet (close to the Swedish Television building at the end of Valhallavägen) as well as in the Olympic Stadium on Vallhallavägen. A few of the main trails around Stockholm are listed below and you can also consult the website *www.skidspar.se* and search your area.

Gärdet
2.5 km long artificial snow track prepared with a piste machine all winter and is free to use.

Stockholm Stadium
Two parallel 400 m long circular tracks.

Lida
Ski trails of between 800 m and 17.9 km, partly lit. Artificial snow on the 800-metre loop, other tracks are prepared when there is enough snow.
www.lida.nu

Ågesta
Ski trails between 500 m and 8.5 km, partly lit trails. Three of the tracks run on the golf course and three follow the lit track in the forests south of Ågesta recreational facility.
www.stockholm.se

Ursvik
Ski trails between 200 m and 15 km, partly lit trails.
www.sundbyberg.se

Hellasgården
Ski trails between 3.5 km and 8.5 km, the shortest is a lit trail. This is also somewhere where you can observe or take part in the extraordinary ritual of having a sauna and then swimming in freezing water in a hole cut out of a lake, *Källtorpssjön*. Bracing, to say the least.
www.hellasgarden.se

Outside Stockholm there are also a number of excellent resorts with fantastic scope for cross-country skiing:

Högbo Bruk
200 km from Stockholm. A total of 50 km of cross-country ski trails, several of which are lit. Official *Vasaloppet* centre where you can book lessons with an instructor. Sales and rental.
www.hogbobruk.se

Orsa Grönklitt
Ski resort at an altitude of 500 metres north of Orsa, 300 km from Stockholm. A total of 80 km tracks, of which 9 km are lit trails. The official Vasaloppet Centre arranges special Vasaloppet camps. Sales and rentals.
www.orsagronklitt.se

Långberget
At an altitude of 630 metres, 450 km from Stockholm. A total of 63 km of prepared tracks, of which 8 km are lit trails. The official *Vasaloppet* Centre arranges *Vasaloppet* camps. Sales and rentals.
www.langberget.se

Further afield are Torsby Skidtunnel, 5 hours from Stockholm near the Norwegian border and the world's longest ski tunnel within a mountain near Östersund. These are excellent if outside conditions are not cold enough for you to practise for extreme races!

What is *Vasaloppet*?

This is the world's biggest annual cross-country ski race which takes place the first Sunday in March. It is 90km (56 miles) long and is inspired by a memorable journey Gustav Eriksson made from Mora to Sälen when he was fleeing from the Danish King Christian II's soldiers during the winter of 1520–1521. He was a Swedish nobleman, who was sheltered and protected by the people of Dalarna who also helped him in his quest to overthrow Kristian II. Gustav Eriksson, better known as Gustav Vasa, was finally crowned King of a free Sweden on 6th June 1523. Four hundred years later, in 1922, the first *Vasaloppet* took place and has continued since with only 3 exceptions. In 1932 and 1990 it was cancelled owing to lack of snow and in 1934 there were too few participants. 2021 it was only open to elite skiers, others were permitted to participate in *Vasaåket* following detailed corona-rules... with at least one pole length's distance.

Once you have mastered cross-country skiing, why not try the ultimate Swedish Classic Circuit (*En Svensk Klassiker)?* It is a diploma awarded to those who have finished races combining the four disciplines of cross-country, swimming, biking and cross country running during a 12-month period. Thousands of people, mostly Swedes, take part in all four each year and receive the Swedish Classic Circuit award.

Other Outdoor Activities

Dog sledding
Another key experience for your stay in Sweden, but do you need to
follow the crowds to Kiruna to experience it? No! Much as Kiruna,
right in the north of Sweden, offers whole holidays centred around
dog sledding, amazing opportunities are also available near Järvsö, 3
hours' drive from Stockholm and near other ski resorts. This is the
most exhilarating experience – fast-paced, elemental, thrilling. You
will sit in a low-slung toboggan behind 7 husky dogs whose only
desire is to move forwards as fast as possible in amazing formation
and go either for a couple of hours with hot chocolate between stops
or on a longer expedition. There is no better way to feel absolutely at
one with the snow, ice, bright winter light and fabulous emptiness of
Sweden. Mushing (driving the toboggan) can also be an option,
giving you a first-hand experience of controlling the dogs and
balancing the toboggan at the same time.

Snöskoter – Snowmobiling
This is a thrilling mode of transport way up
north during the winter months. You can enjoy
tailored snowmobile safaris including
wilderness lunches, dinner in Sami teepees,
saunas, hot tubs, mountain lodges, campfires,
ice fishing - don't forget your thermal
underwear!

Ice Driving
For car enthusiasts, have you ever heard of ice driving? For anyone
with an interest in cars this is a once in a lifetime experience! You get
to drive on specially prepared ice tracks on a frozen lake in rally cars
fitted with studded tyres. Lapland has the world's best winter testing
environment and every winter Arjeplog becomes the European
capital of extreme condition car testing.
www.driversparadise.se
www.icedriving.net

Gardens, Flora and Fauna

Gardens and islands to visit

Although gardening itself is fairly challenging given Stockholm's northerly position, there are some lovely gardens to visit along the lines of the Swedish idyll of sitting under an apple tree eating delicious cake. The best places to do this are Rosendals Trädgård on Djurgården where there is a delightful café and plants for sale, or by visiting the fabulous garden centre at Ulriksdal *(www.rappne.se)* which is a sight for sore eyes as winter ends, with its massive array of plants and bulbs available from its glasshouses. In summer you can also cut wild flowers from their gardens and pay by weight. The café is excellent too.

For a more detailed gardening visit, go to Bergianska Trädgården *(www.bergianska.se)* which has well laid out gardens, an excellent glasshouse with lots of specimen plants and a wonderful café to enjoy lunch, as well as walks by the water. Or, more specialised still and further afield are the gardens of Carl Linnaeus, the father of modern taxonomy (the classification of organisms) in Uppsala where there is a full reconstruction of Linnaeus' botanical garden as it would have been in the 18th century.

Walking takes on a whole new complexion in spring in Sweden. It is a poignantly brief season and oh, so welcome after the very long winter, with its veritable eruption of masses of wildflowers which you will find in woods, forests and meadows everywhere. One of the very best places to enjoy this is the glorious island of Ängsö, Europe's first national park and a haven of nature at its best. Go in mid-May to enjoy carpets of anemones, primula and the very special Adam and Eve wild orchids. Something not to be missed.

www.nationalparksofsweden.se click on 'choose park' and then go to the end of the list and click on 'Ängsö'.

Another option is the island of Gällnö in the archipelago, which has ancient fields aglow with yellow primula dancing in the wind – just gorgeous and testament to how Sweden has kept close to the ancient rites of nature and the seasons.

Swedish flowers

You cannot help but be inspired by the wealth of wild flowers in Sweden, which make you feel as if you have stepped back into a more old-fashioned, untainted world. You will also notice that shrubs in Sweden grow in almost wild profusion – very different to the well-pruned, micro-managed specimens in the UK or elsewhere (or attempts at such!). So take the opportunity to appreciate what is all around you.

In spring, it's true that you will have to be extremely patient, as only the bravest of wildflowers will emerge in late April before a veritable eruption in May. The main flowers to look for are:

- *Liten Blåklocka* (Sweden's national flower – campanula rotundifolia)
- *Blåsippor* (blue anemones)
- *Vitsippa* (wood / white anemones)
- *Kungsängslilja* (snakeshead fritillaria)
- *Adam och Eva* (Adam and Eve orchids)
- *Styvmorsviol* (violets)
- *Gullviva* (primula)
- *Scilla* (scilla)
- *Tussilago* (coltsfoot or butterbur)

In late May, don't miss the explosion of cherry blossom on Stockholm's Kungsträdgården – it is a fabulous sight, but keep your ear to the ground as it is a fleeting wonder and if it's windy, may last only a few days. The gardens around Berzelli Park have wonderful displays of tulips and Imperial fritillaria in May / June in a riot of stunning colours.

On summer evenings, take the opportunity to get out on your bike after supper to luxuriate in the beautiful light and, in May and June, balmy smells of amelanchier, lilac or *rosa rugosa*. Or revel in fields of bright blue cornflowers.

Swedish trees

63% of Sweden is covered in forest and much of this is pine, whilst the birch tree also features prominently and the Ornäs birch, a variety of silver birch with deeply indented leaves, is the national tree of Sweden. The oak tree has also played a very important role in Swedish history, being planted specifically to facilitate shipbuilding – everything from the ill-fated *Vasa* to a host of other ships and boats in this seafaring nation. You may find that the dark colour palette of Sweden's trees has you crying out for views over one of its 96,000 lakes, but that said, the forest is very much at the heart of many a Swede's well-being. Certainly the vast scale of the country's forests is incredible.

Animals – the rare and wonderful

Most famous amongst Sweden's animals is undoubtedly the moose (*älg*), which you may also find referred to as elk. This is a point of some confusion, but what's clear is that moose are solitary, awe-inspiring beasts who roam happily in Sweden in the greatest numbers per square kilometre of any country in the world. Now that's a rare claim! In practice, other than at Skansen you are very unlikely to see one, but if you feel a large beast coming up behind you with an extraordinarily protuberant nose and a back almost 2 metres off the ground, it will be a moose. But fear not - they are much more likely to potter undisturbed in the forest with their almost 400,000 fellow moose. This number falls in the autumn, when up to 100,000 are shot by hunters, to be replaced by another 100,000 calves the following spring.

Otherwise, Sweden has a number of animals in relative profusion which are a much rarer sight elsewhere. Red squirrels are fairly easy to see and an absolute delight. They are vulnerable to their less rarefied grey cousins, but it is magical to see these beautiful creatures darting about amongst the trees in search of berries and excitement, the signature bushy tail swishing as they go. Hares are also a common sight in Sweden, particularly in the morning where you may see small congregations in fields.

Sweden's rarer animals include the bear, Arctic fox, wolverine, lynx, beaver and wolf. You can see all of these at close quarters at either Skansen (in the city) or Järvzoo north of Stockholm. Or if you're very keen to see these creatures in their natural habitat, try a wildlife adventure with *www.wildsweden.com*. Or if seals are your thing, visit the wonderful seal colonies in Koster National Park on Sweden's west coast (*www.naturesbestsweden.com*) or even closer in Stockholm be adventurous and board a rib-boat that will take you way out to the barren outer archipelago to see the seals - this is a year round adventure.
www.oppethav.se

Sweden's prize bird is the golden eagle. Enough said.

Learning Swedish

Language, finding your feet and reading between the lines
Swedish is undeniably a complicated language, chiefly in terms of pronunciation, and Swedes speak English of an astonishingly high level. This might easily lead you to think that there is little point in learning Swedish and while it's true that you can get by with very little in areas around Stockholm, further afield this is less the case. And what's more, you're living with Swedes and the effort made in learning even some of the language will pay back handsomely in bringing you closer to Swedish people, getting more of an insight into Swedish culture and demonstrating your willingness to accept the challenge and make a positive gesture. If you have learned any German before, then you will find vocabulary less difficult as many words have similar roots – and you will be reassured to discover that, broadly speaking, Swedish grammar is easier than German.

As mentioned above, some Swedish will help enormously in the workplace and in many situations it will be essential. It is also crucial to be able to understand particular set phrases – when ringing the doctor, taking someone to hospital or just ordering in a restaurant or bar. Not to mention extremely complicated forms you will need to fill in if completing a tax return, car insurance or similar. So it will pay to make a start anyway.

Depending on where you are living, you may find yourself in an area with many expats, such as around BISS (British International School of Stockholm) in Danderyd / Djursholm. Or your job may require you to speak much more Swedish.

Firstly, you need a good teacher. There is obviously a wide choice, but a few companies come highly recommended:

Lidgard Education
Run by Cecilia Lidgard who has worked as a management consultant and banker as an expat in the UK, US, France and Madrid, provides Swedish language classes really tailored to the needs of expats. She

teaches at all levels and, with a close awareness of issues facing people in a new country, also runs workshops on how to optimise the experience of living abroad and make the most of the positives. She can also help with cross-cultural awareness with an emphasis on reading between the lines and understanding what is really meant by what people say. *www.lidgardeducation.com*

Swedish for Professionals
The goal of their courses and workshops is to help international professionals integrate effectively into Sweden and communicate in Swedish for business and leisure purposes. Their Swedish courses are fun, engaging and innovative and allow participants to pick a day and time to fit in with their busy schedules.
www.swedishforprofessional.com

New in Sweden
For really practical and supportive insights into how to set yourself up in Sweden, find your feet and network with local small business owners too, New in Sweden is an invaluable resource. There is also a dedicated section – New in Danderyd – with specific information on the Danderyd area which is home to so many expats living near Stockholm. Run by marketing expert Zennie Holmgren, a Brit married to a Swede, the focus is on providing Swedish language workshops on particular topics, offering advice on the practicalities of living in Sweden and, through sister website *www.writeindanderyd.com*, facilitating marketing and networking for small businesses. *www.newinsweden.com*

Tree Coaching
Run by Helen Lettinga, who is Dutch but has lived abroad for 9 years, Tree Coaching offers personal coaching to help with career development, family relationships and approaching the challenges and opportunities of living abroad. She also runs workshops on positive personal development and communication. Really helpful for getting things in perspective and seeing the way forward.
www.tree-coaching.com

A Quick Swedish Lesson

In order to get going with the Swedish language it will help to understand that particular consonants make other consonants soft when pronounced and that Swedish has three extra vowels - å, ä, ö – which will need some practising and contortion of your mouth to sound right! These are added to the list of vowels, along with y, making a total of nine vowels.

A is pronounced differently depending on whether it is long or short. It is pronounced like the 'a' in car when long. If short, it sounds more like 'u' in but.

E is pronounced like the 'e' in deck, and when long more like the 'ea' in real.

I is pronounced like the 'i' in sin. When long, it's like the 'ea' in mean.

O can be pronounced in two different ways. It can sound like the 'oo' in hoot, or it can be pronounced like the 'o' in the word hot.

U is quite a difficult vowel as there is no sound in English exactly like it. The closest example would be the long 'o' sounds in the English words who and you. Somewhere in between the 'u' in humour and the 'o' in Homer.

Y is another difficult one where there is no sound in English quite like it. Try pronouncing the English letter 'e' then elongating your lips outwards as if taking a selfie with 'duck lips'!

Å as in the 'o' in the word four.

Ä as in the 'ai' in the English word hair.

Ö as in the 'u' in the word urn.

It is important to really practise these vowels. Swedes will not be able to understand you if you cannot grasp Swedish pronunciation and remember to talk slowly. Consonants are mostly the same, but there are a few differences

J sounds like the 'y' in yes.

K sounds like the 'k' in keep or the 'sh' in sheep.
R is rolled, but not too forcefully.
S is like the 's' in soft.

Then we come to the impossible '*sj-ljud*' or sh-sound which is quite a mouthful and varies depending on where you come from in Sweden. An example is the word for biscuits or crackers – *kex*. If you are from Gothenburg you will pronounce it *shex* and if you are in Stockholm you would say *kex*.

The sh sound has many variations in its spelling as well as its pronunciation – you will need a Swede to help you out with these but here are some examples:

SK as in *skära*
SJ as in *själ*
SCH as in *schema*
STJ as in *stjärna*
SKJ as in *skjorta*
CH as in *chaufför*
TI as in *station*
SI as in *television*
GE as in *generös*
GI as in *giraff*
GIÖ as in *religiös*
RS as in *Lars*
TS as in *hurts*

Thirdly, it is well worth getting to grips with some basics early on and building from there:

Greetings
- Hello - *Hej hej!*
- How are you - *Hur mår du?*
- Thank you – *Tack, tack.*
- Thank you very much - *Tack så mycket.*
- Sorry/Excuse me – *Förlåt.*

- Excuse me - *Ursäkta*

In a café
- Can I have a cup of coffee, please? - *Kan jag be att få en kopp kaffe, tack?*
- A cinnamon bun - *En kanelbulle*
- Some milk and sugar please - *Lite mjölk och socker, tack*
- Can I pay please - *Kan jag få betala, tack?*
- How much does it cost - *Vad kostar det?*

In a shop
- Please can I have a receipt? - *Kvittot, tack?*
- How much is it? - *Vad kostar det?*

At the doctor's
- Prescription - *Recept*
- Appointment - *Tid*
- Immunisation/Vaccination - *Immunisering/Vaccination*
- Flu vaccination - *Influensavaccin*
- Nurse - *Sjuksköterska*
- Designated doctor - *Husläkare*
- General Practitioner - *Allmänläkare*
- Referral to a specialist - *Remiss till specialist*

It's true to say that a few words go a long way and will help you feel more at home. Also, Swedish has the great advantage of having a number of words which are used extremely frequently, so if you can master these you will quickly feel as though you're making progress:

- *Bra* - great
- *Tack* – thank you
- *Tack so mycket* – thank you very much
- *Vad kul* – how cool, great, excellent
- *Vad roligt* – ah that's funny, classic

- *Absolut* – exactly, I agree
- *Precis* – quite, I agree

Some odd Swedish words which are useful to know to avoid misunderstandings

- *bra* – it simply means 'good' and is not a part of the female wardrobe
- *kiss* – urine
- *puss* – kiss
- *kock* – chef (so, Swedish chef is *svensk kock* in Swedish)
- *fart–* speed
- *fack, facket* or *fackförening* – union, trade union
- *sex* – six
  Swedes say sex when they talk about the number 6. Strangely, they also say sex when they mean *sex.*
- *slut* - finish(ed), that's enough

There are also some great apps that you can use to learn Swedish, such as Duolingo and once you advance to the next level you can download an app called *SVT Språkplay.* We explain this in more detail in the chapter about 'Keeping up to date', as you use the app in connection with watching Swedish television programmes.

Social Life & Customs

Swedes are renowned for being very friendly, but this should be qualified. They are often extremely self-reliant people, perhaps partly because of the tough climate and also because they tend to feel they should fend for themselves. People can often feel very different about social interaction in the winter versus the summer. So be prepared for people who don't necessarily 'need' you and who may well not feel welcoming at first. Swedes are also sparing with their language, so don't expect the exuberant welcome you might receive from a Spaniard or Italian. Furthermore, Swedes often form a tight group of friends early on in life and stick to them, so they may not be in need of making friends at work or with newcomers.

It makes sense to join in with the Swedish way of doing things in order to make friends and interact. Speaking the language is a great first step, as is spending time on Swedish pursuits. This will provide common ground with Swedes and ease contact, as well as helping you make the very most of some of the unique opportunities Sweden has to offer. So, think about joining an ice hockey team in the winter, going skating on frozen lakes near you, coaching football for your local team, getting involved with sailing. It's noticeable that young people are given a lot of responsibility for coaching and clubs, so you can really help make a difference. Or demonstrating an interest in seasonal things will help you have common ground with neighbours – learn how to pick chanterelles, enjoy amazing autumn colours on long walks....more on this below.

At a Swedish home
If you are invited to dinner with Swedish friends, be prepared for a number of particular things. Firstly, you must arrive on time – that is just the norm. Then, be ready to take off your shoes on arrival – this can be slightly off putting if you have holes in your socks or tights! You will normally always take off your outdoor shoes in the hall and then walk around in your socks. However, despite Sweden boasting about its equality there is a 'class' distinction here which is not always easy for a foreigner to gauge (or a Swede for that matter)!

So, to play it safe, <u>always</u> take an extra pair of proper indoor shoes (not slippers) with you. That way you will never be wrong and can change into these when you arrive. Swedes do not like bringing the snow or dirt from outside into their houses. It's also perfectly normal to take off outdoor winter boots when you arrive at a smarter restaurant, too, and change into your indoor shoes.

It is customary to bring a small present or flowers. If you have brought flowers they will most probably be well wrapped in thick paper (often to protect against the cold). This paper should be removed just before you arrive at the door.

When you are offered a drink, you should wait until all the guests have one and the host or hostess has made a toast, until you can take a sip, having raised your glass to all the guests around the table. At the table, if you are sitting on the right hand side of the hostess, you may be expected to make a toast and speech in her honour at the end of the main course (mentioning the delicious dinner).

Swedes are rightly proud of their beautiful country and will be touched by you showing your interest in and appreciation of it. People tend towards being reserved and undemonstrative, so be aware of this and fit in accordingly. That said, Swedes also love drinking songs and if you're celebrating Midsummer, eating crayfish in August or at a birthday party, then there may be singing well into the night.

Social conduct in public places tends to be quiet and unobtrusive too. So, if you are walking, running or cycling, it is polite to acknowledge another person with a brief 'Hej hej', but do not necessarily expect an answer, particularly if it's snowing. There are some theories that because Sweden has so much space, people are unused to having others in their personal space, so you may walk down a pavement or hotel corridor and find someone walking straight into you. This is not rude – just that they didn't expect anyone else to be there!

Given very strong equality between the sexes, do not expect a man to hold the door for you if you're female, let you go in first or carry anything heavy for you. He would be fearful of insulting you and the extent of womens' liberation in Sweden makes this sort of thing frowned upon.

Dinner etiquette
There are any number of subtle rules but some of the most important are to arrive on time, toast each other before drinking, make a speech if sitting on the right of the hostess, and be prepared for drinking songs.

Having a smoke after dinner has nearly disappeared from the party scene and if people have a cigarette, they will do so outdoors. There are designated public areas in cities where smoking is permitted but it is prohibited in playgrounds, bus and railway stations, and in outdoor sections of restaurants and bars.

However, you may have noticed some Swedes walking around with a slight bulging upper lip. No? Look again! They are using *snus* which is a moist, smokeless tobacco often packaged into small pouches (like tiny tea bags) in round boxes that are kept refrigerated. For the real *snus* enthusiast, the most common term for a pinch of *snus* is *prilla* and loose *snus* is preferred. It can be blended into your own favourite taste, either coarse, medium or finely ground and you roll it into a ball or *prilla* in your hand and place it under your upper lip. Don't be surprised if someone at the table discreetly takes out their *snus* after dinner - they might even offer you some!

If you want to discover more about this habit that evolved from the 16th century snuff, you can visit the Swedish Match shop on Kungsgatan 3 in Stockholm. Here you can blend your own taste or ask them to show you the oldest (from 1822) of their brands, *Ettan*.

How to toast

Regardless of the toast, lift the glass with your right hand. It should be held about 10 cm below the Adam's Apple. Sometimes the glass can be lifted a little higher to chin height in tribute. Keep the glass at a reasonable distance in front of you. Aim the glass at the person you are referring to and keep eye contact. Always toast with a smile.

Nowadays, everyone can toast everyone, man to woman, woman to man and younger to older. There are other stricter rules however, if you are invited to attend a Royal dinner or the Nobel Banquet. A male guest is expected to toast his table partner who is the person to the right of him and then the person sitting to the left of him, as well as the person opposite (if they are sitting nearby).

If you are a small group (6 or less) and you wish to be formal, you are also expected to toast the hostess - if you were a larger group the hostess would quickly get very drunk if she was being toasted by everyone!

Should you happen to be sitting to the left of the hostess you are expected to hold a thank-you-for-the-delicious-dinner-speech! This is normally done towards the end of the dinner or with the dessert.

If you are at a dinner and dance party, the man sitting to your left is supposed to dance the first dance with you - thereafter it is free for all. Generally and at formal dinners, you will never be seated next to your spouse - there is one exception to this rule and that is if you are newly engaged.

Keeping Up To Date

As well as having your colleagues, friends and neighbours as a source of local news, there are some other useful resources available.

The Local
The Local online newspaper covers all current local news including events, politics, business, sports and culture and is the best place for keeping up to date. The Local started its online newspaper in Stockholm and now also provides English-language digital local news to readers in Austria, Denmark, France, Germany, Italy, Norway, Spain and Switzerland. It has a very active book club too.
www.thelocal.se

Mundus International
Another newspaper is Mundus International, which provides in depth news and analysis of Swedish current affairs. Their online publications include Mundus Business Insights, Mundus News, Mundus Weekly & the Monthly Policy Review.
www.mundus-international.com

SR & SVT
Sveriges Radio or Radio Sweden is Sweden's official international broadcasting station. It is a non-commercial and politically independent public service broadcasting company. They carry the latest news from Sweden during business hours from Monday to Friday on the web and on social media. You can find all their reports and podcasts in Swedish Radio's own app 'Sveriges Radio Play'. They also have two podcasts:

Radio Sweden Daily is a short wrap-up of Sweden's top stories (4:30 pm Monday - Friday).

Radio Sweden Weekly is an in-depth 30-minute programme on Thursdays at 4.30 pm. It also broadcasts on the P2 and P6 FM stations across Sweden, with a repeat on Mondays.
www.sverigesradio.se/radiosweden

Don't rule out Swedish Television as a source of information or entertainment. *Sveriges Television* (SVT) is the Swedish public service television funded by a tax on personal income, so you might be paying for it anyway - why not benefit! Foreign series and films are generally never dubbed so SVT is an excellent resource of high quality, English speaking films – and without incessant interruptions from commercials. SVT's digital platform is called SVTplay.
www.svtplay.se/

Children's programmes are great to follow as a way of learning a new language and *Sveriges Television* has come up with a fabulous new way to learn Swedish - *SVT Språkplay*!

As mentioned in the chapter 'Learning Swedish', having mastered Duolingo we suggest you download the *SVT Språkplay* app. This can only be done from Sweden. The app is free for those who would like to learn more Swedish and watch TV at the same time and offers subtitled TV programmes (in Swedish) with interactive language support into 25 languages. *SVT Språkplay* can be used on your mobile device and on TV using Chromecast. They also have an app called *Språkkraft Läscoach* which allows you to learn the Swedish language whilst reading daily media content from the Swedish media.

Soaking Up The Seasons

Winter can be up to 6 months, spring is extremely short, summer is long and languid, autumn is a brief prelude to another winter but very beautiful. Tourist places are open for a very short period of time in summer – make sure you don't miss them! Key places to go per season include:

Winter
- Skiing – Romme, places local to Stockholm, Åre
- Skating on lakes – Norrviken, Edsviken, in Stockholm
- Cross-country skiing
- Dog sledding – near Järvsö
- *Julbord*
- Lucia
- Gamla Stan Christmas market and others in *slotts* (e.g. near Mariefred)
- Millesgården in the snow
- Lunchtime concerts at the Opera
- Royal Palace
- Butterfly house at Hagaparken
- *Tekniska Museet* with children

Spring
- Ängsö
- Cherry blossom in Kungsträdgården
- Cycle along the water to soak up the smells of spring / summer
- *Valborg* bonfires and ceremonies
- *Fotografiska Museet*
- Drottningholm
- Sigtuna
- Ulriksdal – lunch, gathering flowers, walking by the lake

- Naturhistoriska Museet
- Skansen

Summer
- The archipelago
- Rent a *stuga* on Grinda
- Discover Vaxholm – gateway to the archipelago and the best cakes
- *Midsommar*
- Boating
- Camping
- Fishing
- Swimming
- *Kräftskiva* (crayfish parties)
- Castles – Skokloster, Rosersberg etc.
- Lunch in *Rosendals Trädgård*
- *Gröna Lund*

Autumn
- Soak up the autumn colours at the Waldemarsudde
- Enjoy the Swedish forest and pick chanterelles
- Tyresö
- Visiting Gripsholm and staying in Maricfred
- Stockholm's highlights – Hallwylska, Stadshuset, tea at Svenskt Tenn, the Vasa, Junibacken, Riddarhuset, Tyska Kyrkan, Gamla Stan, dinner at Eriks Gondolen
- Artipelag
- The Post Museum in Gamla Stan (young children)
- The '*Polkagris*' shop which shows the red and white stripy sugar canes being made – in Gamla Stan

The Swedish Year

There are very distinct seasons in Sweden with particular highlights that are a great way of getting beneath the skin of the country and shouldn't be missed.

January

13th January

In Sweden there is a saying - "*tjugondag Knut kastas granen ut*" - which means that on St Knut's day it is time to throw out the Christmas tree. Sometimes parties are held with some singing and dancing before the tree is sent for recycling - check how and where from your neighbours.

Vikingarännet

The world's longest annual skating race on natural ice! This is a popular yearly ice-skating event held late in January or beginning of February. The start is in Uppsala (80 km track) or Sigtuna (35 km track) with the finish in Kungsängen (ice conditions permitting).
www.vikingarannet.com

If it has been a mild winter and the ice hasn't frozen everywhere on Lake Mälaren, then you might like to check *Sigtunarännet* on:
www.sigtunarannet.se

Ice Skating in and around Stockholm

Östermalms IP (Fiskartorpsvägen 2 - next door to Stadion) is open daily and here you can rent ice skates or try your long distance ice skates - it is never too late to start! You can try skating on natural ice on lakes around Stockholm such as Kottlasjön on Lidingö or at Hellasgården. Make sure you have the necessary safety equipment with you.

Skiing near Stockholm
There are a number of places you can ski very close to Stockholm, both downhill and cross country. More details about this can be found under the Winter Sports section.

February/March

Fettisdagen - Shrove Tuesday
Renowned for the wonderful choice of delicious buns that we eat. You will most probably already find them on the shelves straight after Christmas! Key names for the same buns are:

- *Fastlagsbulle*
- *Fettisdagsbulle* (literally, Shrove Tuesday buns)
- *Semla*

A good time for *fika* and coffee. Why not try a sprinkle of cardamom in your coffee? This is the world's third most expensive spice by weight after saffron and vanilla and is used a lot in Swedish baking. The seeds smell heavenly when crushed in a pestle and mortar, or food mixer.

March

25th March *Våffeldagen* or *Vårfrudagen* – Waffle Day
The Annunciation Day of the Virgin Mary (*Jungfru Marie Bebådelsedag*) which is 9 months before Christmas. The name *Våffeldagen* comes from *Vårfrudagen* (Our Lady's Day) which in vernacular Swedish sounds almost similar.

You will need a waffle iron *(våffeljärn)*, which can usually be bought in your local supermarket at this time of the year. They are not very pricey, ranging from SEK 150 upwards. To make your own waffle mixture, see our recipes.

Easter – *Påsk*

Easter in Sweden has become an increasingly secular celebration. In old fables, on *Skärtorsdagen* (Maundy Thursday) witches flew off on their broomsticks to *Blåkulla* to feast with the devil. Nowadays, children dress up as witches and go door to door saying *'Glad Påsk'* hoping for generous offerings of sweets/candy from their neighbours. The family gathers in homes decorated with birch stems with colourful feathers attached. The food is quite similar to that at Christmas but somewhat lighter – herring and eggs are a prerequisite. The Christmas drink *Julmust* conveniently changes its name to *Påskmust* for Easter! The date for Easter varies and is dependent on the lunar position and the spring equinox but falls sometime between 22nd March and 25th April.

April

1st April - April Fools' Day!

In Sweden we say "*april, april din dumma sill*" when someone has had a trick played on them (April, April you silly herring!).

30th April *Valborgsmässoafton* - Walpurgis

Join the rest of the Swedes by the bonfire and celebrate the arrival of spring! Bonfires take place in many towns and villages. This is a really atmospheric occasion and heralds the beginning of social interaction again after a long winter. Bonfires can reach epic proportions – mind your hair!

30ᵗʰ April The Birthday of H. M. King Carl XVI Gustaf
The Royal Family meets the public at the Outer Courtyard of Stockholm's Royal Palace.

May

1ˢᵗ May – May Day
May Day is a holiday and there are political marches in the cities. Avoid taking the car into the centre of town!

Mothers' Day
(2ⁿᵈ Sunday in May)
Mothers' Day does not have its roots in religion, as in some other countries, but is a reason to spoil the maternal head of the family and perhaps give her a present too.

Gärdesloppet - Prince Bertil Memorial
If you are interested in vintage cars, don't miss this rally around Djurgården each year in May.

June

Studenten - Graduation
This is the time when students graduate from school and you will hear and see many truckloads of youth circling around the centre of Stockholm, blasting out music! Stay clear of the 'beer spray'!

6ᵗʰ June - Swedish National Day
Gustav Vasa became King of Sweden on 6ᵗʰ June 1523 and on 6ᵗʰ June 1809 Sweden adopted a new constitution. There are some local festivities but *Skansen* would be the place to go for good atmosphere with a Royal touch.
www.skansen.se

Midsummer Eve
(falls on the Friday between 19th and 25th June)
This is when we welcome the summer and dance around the maypole
(adorned with leaves and flowers) after which we brave the outdoors
eating herring and fresh potatoes, singing and drinking *snaps* until
the early hours! A wonderful opportunity to soak up the Swedish love
of nature and celebrate in good old-
fashioned style.

You can celebrate Midsummer at
Skansen - for more information
check their website. There will be
events to celebrate Midsummer all
over the place. Particularly
traditional ones are to be found in
the Dalarna region which is well-
known for its maypole dancing and
traditional costumes.
www.skansen.se

July

Summer holidays!
July is the month when most Swedes take their summer holiday. This
is a time when 'business Sweden' comes to a halt! Enjoy the sun and
warmth and if possible, do like the Swedes and rent a lovely little
stuga near the sea. If you stay at home, you will find that many
restaurants and some shops may be closed in more residential areas.
It's also a good time to lock up your house carefully, as thieves can
prey on empty neighbourhoods.

August

Crayfish time
Don your party hats and join the rest of the Swedes as they devour
these bright red crustaceans! Good table manners are largely
abandoned, giving way to lots of singing and *snaps*.

Surströmming time

This is also the time to try *surströmming* (fermented herring). Make sure you open the tin outdoors and if it is your first time trying this northern delicacy, ask a Swede how it should be eaten.

On the third Thursday in August there are 2 restaurants in Stockholm serving this delicacy - book a table at Sturehof or Tennstopet or just walk past for the smell of it!
www.sturehof.com
www.tennstopet.se

September

Running challenges

For the *Tjemilen* race, 28,000 female runners and joggers of all ages run 10,000 metres from Gärdet through Djurgården Royal park in central Stockholm.

On the last weekend in September, there is *Lidingöloppet*, the world's largest cross-country race with more than 44,000 participants.

Autumn fair

The *Skansen* Autumn Fair takes place at the end of September. Meet tavern waitresses, stable-lads, farmers and farmhands bringing this year's produce to the market.

Mushroom picking time

The mushroom hunting season also begins. There are a few varieties of mushroom that are easily recognisable of which the most common is probably the *trattkantarell* (chanterelle) with its beautiful golden caramel colouring. You should never eat anything you have doubts about and are advised to consult a guidebook or app if unsure or go foraging with a knowledgeable Swede. Mushrooms like to hide but once you have located one there should be many nearby. Check around trees and in the moss in wooded areas.

October

4th October *Kanelbullens Dag* – Cinnamon Bun Day
This is the day when the whole of Sweden smells of cinnamon buns! They will feature at breakfast in hotels and of course at *fika* in the office. More than 8 million buns are sold on this day.

Halloween (not traditionally a Swedish custom)
Halloween is obviously on 31st October. Note that whilst it is growing in popularity and some children go from door to door asking for '*bus eller godis*' (trick or treat), many Swedes feel uncomfortable at it falling just before the peace and sanctitude of All Saints Day. So tread carefully and perhaps celebrate Halloween just within school, with a small group of friends or a few days later.

November

Allhelgonsdagen - All Saints Day
(falls on the Saturday between 31st October and 6th November)
This is the day when Swedes visit relatives' graves and light candles by their gravestones. It is well worth visiting one of the graveyards at dusk – many Swedish graveyards are much closer to nature than in other countries and often have wonderful trees and plants, so this is a beautiful sight with all the candles burning!

Fathers' Day
(2nd Sunday in November)
Imported from America many years ago, this is really a chance to spend some family time and spoil fathers with a present.

11th November *Mårten Gås* - St Martin's Day
This is mostly celebrated in the south of Sweden, in Skåne. It is really to mark the end of the agricultural year but has become a reason to indulge in eating rich goose.

December

Probably the busiest month in Sweden.

1ˢᵗ December - Winter Tyres

During the period from 1ˢᵗ December to 31ˢᵗ March, winter tyres are required in Sweden, if the road conditions demand it. Many people put them on in advance.

Advent

A candle is lit on each Sunday in Advent with a final candle on Christmas Day. This is the time to buy a Christmas tree and get out all your Christmas decorations. Swedes are very keen on candles and you will see them adorning windows throughout December. Decorations tend to be taken down on 13ᵗʰ January while singing the traditional frog dance song *Små Grodorna* in more traditional settings or hotels. A great way of learning Swedish is to follow the children's Christmas *Adventskalender* on Swedish Television (SVT1). Each year they have a new series of 24 episodes culminating in the last on Christmas Day.

Christmas Markets

Swedish Christmas markets are really charming and full of beautiful decorations, with Father Christmas' *Tomtar* featuring prominently, as well as delicious seasonal food for your *Julbord* or Christmas lunch. There is a lovely range of markets to choose between, from the iconic market in Stockholm's *Gamla Stan* to *Elfviksgård* on Lidingö, to a special archipelago market experience on the island of Utö. Or you can choose fabulous markets at beautiful castles, most notably Taxinge Slott near Mariefred or Steninge Slott near Sigtuna.

10ᵗʰ December – The Nobel Day

The Nobel Laureates receive their Nobel medals from King Carl XVI Gustaf of Sweden at a special ceremony in the Concert Hall where the Royals don their finest tiaras and jewels, followed by the banquet dinner held in the Blue Hall at the Stockholm City Hall. As laureates are allowed to bring a number of their relations, it's a great time for people spotting in Stockholm! Keep an eye out at the Grand Hotel which is where they all stay. It is not unusual for Swedes to have their own Nobel celebration dinner at home whilst watching the real thing live on TV.

You might wonder why the Peace prize ceremony is held in Oslo and not in Sweden like the rest of the prizes. We don't quite know why Alfred Nobel decided that only the Peace prize should be awarded by a committee in Norway, but when writing his will in Paris, Norway was still in union with Sweden under the same king. The other prizes were to be awarded by appropriate committees in Sweden and in Norway the Peace Prize was to be awarded by a committee chosen by the Norwegian Parliament.

13th December - *Lucia*
Lucia is celebrated across Sweden in schools, churches and offices. There is a wonderful choice of places to see this gorgeous and truly Scandinavian event. At school, every child will dress up as either a *tomte* (Father Christmas), *pepparkaksgubbe* or *pepparkaksgumma* (gingerbreadman) or *stjärngosse* (a star boy) and they will come home singing a range of stunning traditional songs in the weeks before the all-important performance. Note that you will need to buy these costumes as soon as they become available in supermarkets, as otherwise stocks can quickly run out. *Skansen* always has a wonderful Lucia ceremony, as does *Storkyrkan* (Stockholm's main cathedral in Gamla Stan).

Rosendals Trädgård has a beautiful concert or the cavalry / mounted guard has a mounted ceremony which is totally different and a wonderful equine display. Check their website and calendar for parades and other events.
www.beridnahogvakten.se

24th December – *Julafton*
Christmas Eve is the main day when Swedes celebrate Christmas. This is one of the biggest celebrations during the year and churches will have a variety of service, some with midnight mass or by candlelight.

25th December – *Juldagen*
On Christmas Day, many churches will celebrate with an early morning *Jullotta* celebrating the nativity of Jesus.

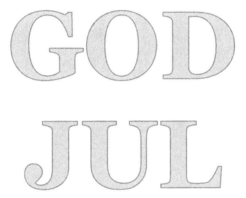

For Children

Stockholm is a fantastic city for children. It is so clean, spacious and full of well-conceived museums which will delight and spur the imagination. People arriving in Sweden from other cities often breathe a sigh of relief at the ease of life with children here – it can feel as if you have gone back several decades in terms of the pace of things, as well as having state-of-the-art technology at the same time. A fantastic combination! Here are some favoured spots for trips with children:

Junibacken

On Djurgården, this has to be the most distinctive and memorable children's museum in Stockholm. It is a simply incredible magical world, where scenes from Sweden's most famous children's classics are brought to life in astonishing detail probably unrivalled anywhere else. It is like the very best doll's house or pirate ship you can imagine and all for children to explore and enjoy. Highlights include replica wooden houses from Sven Nordqvist's *Pettson and Findus* books with every detail and eccentric cat and chicken reproduced to perfection. Then upstairs, Pippi Longstocking's Villa Villekulla replete with a life-size model of her horse. Perhaps the most entrancing thing is the captivating train ride which takes you on a journey through some of Sweden's best known childrens' stories, with those of Astrid Lindgren looming large. The scenes of these are depicted with exquisitely crafted models and houses, with no attention to detail spared, as you pass through idyllic Swedish country summer scenes and highlights of Stockholm's rooftops. Be warned that there is a large rat with livid red eyes who pops out at one point and that the story of Astrid Lindgren's own son's death is also portrayed in typically unsentimental Swedish style. But this is a really illuminating experience and a season ticket is a really compelling investment for younger children.

Post Museum

Situated in Gamla Stan in what was, until 1869, Stockholm's only post office, the Post Museum is quite simply entrancing. It displays a fascinating history of the postal service in Sweden showing how postmen have grappled with incredibly difficult climate conditions since the 17th century to deliver the post against all odds, including a range of different post vans up to the present day. But the real highlight is the *Lilla Posten* (Little Post Office) downstairs, where children can get behind the steering wheel of the post van, take part in every part of delivery from the immaculate replica of a sorting office to the adorable miniature versions of Stockholm streets, replete with little houses and post boxes. You can also design your own letter and have it posted to anywhere in Sweden. The whole experience is totally absorbing and perfect for a winter's afternoon. *www.postmuseum.se*

Tekniska Museet
(National Museum of Science and Technology)
This museum is really magnetic and beautifully conceived. At its most traditional, it houses a perfectly rendered model train track from the 1950s with more than 50 metres of track moving through an immaculately built landscape and tunnels. It has superb exhibits showcasing mechanics, light, sound and time in a vibrant area perfectly suited to younger children. And at its most modern, it has fantastic displays about the digital world, a radio station and 1,000 square metres of game stations and environments. There is also much to explain how Sweden's skill for innovation has developed over time. Another excellent spot on a cold or wet afternoon and near to a range of other museums in this part of Djurgården. *www.tekniskamuseet.se*

Police Museum
Very close to the Tekniska Museet is the Polismuseet, a small but fun museum the highlight of which is probably the area designed for younger children which has uniforms to try on and – most gripping of all – a miniature police car in which hours of fun can be spent. *www.polismuseet.se*

Maritime Museum
Also close to the technology and police museums is the Sjöhistoriska, which gives an excellent overview of Sweden's maritime past and

present. It has everything from a host of model boats, beautiful paintings and naval uniforms, detonators and full size beautifully restored boats, to entire icebreakers. Visit to get a feel for just how important the water is to Sweden's history and identity.
www.sjohistoriska.se

The *Vasa*
The story of the *Vasa*, the world's best preserved 17th century ship, is the stuff of legend in Stockholm. Its mast, emerging from the roof of the museum built specially to house it, dominates Djurgården's skyline from Östermalm or Gamla Stan. Embodying Sweden's imperial prowess during the Great Power Era of that time, she set off on her maiden voyage in August 1628 laden with 64 cannons but would capsize almost immediately, top heavy as she was and with inadequate ballast having been built into the bottom of the ship to make her float securely. It is a truly astonishing sight in a museum brilliantly conceived to show each layer of the ship to best advantage and really bringing both the vessel and its doomed history to life. Don't miss the excellent film before you look at the ship itself – the story of how it emerged from 333 years of darkness in 1961 is amazing. You will find yourself returning to the Vasa again and again, so magnetic is its pull and tragic its fate.
www.vasamuseet.se

The Royal Stables & Changing of the Guard
The immaculately kept Royal Stables provide a serene scene in mid Östermalm – you step off the street into a timeless world of equine calm. The 20 horses are perfectly trained to take part in processions and cortèges for state visits and other Royal occasions. These are extremely happy horses, trained daily in spacious Djurgården and put out to meadows in the summer and a delight to see.
www.kungligaslotten.se

You can hear them trotting down Strandvägen and towards the Royal Palace to assist with the Changing of the Guard, which alternates between a walking or mounted ceremony. This takes place on weekdays at 12.15p.m. in the Royal courtyard to the rear of the palace and at 1.15p.m. on Sundays. It is worth arriving a little early to get a good vantage point and the ceremony takes about 20 minutes.

ArkDes - the museum of architecture and design
(the annual Gingerbread House Competition)
In late November on the tranquil island of Skeppsholmen, right in the middle of Stockholm, is filled with a truly irresistible smell – gingerbread! This is a fiercely fought competition with a different theme each year and categories for children, adults and professional architects / designers and the results are nothing short of sensational. Every structure is built of gingerbread, with every sort of edible decoration imaginable. This is possibly the most original and endearing exhibition you will see – lasting until early January, it is definitely worth not leaving your visit too late as the creations can sag a bit as the weeks move on. Just stunning.
www.arkdes.se

Stockholm Toy Museum
Still on the island of Skeppsholmen, but this time underground, you can visit *Bergrummet* and the Stockholm Toy Museum. This is Northern Europe's largest collection of toys and comics. With digital technology combined with a creative team of prop makers and scenographers they have created an inspiring visual experience to suit visitors of all ages.
www.toymuseum.se

Gamla Stans Polkagriskokeri
Red and white stripy candy sticks are synonymous with Christmas tree decorations and the sweet-toothed in Sweden, and this is the place to see them made. The sticks are made before your eyes all day every day and you can even take part in a workshop. This is traditional artistry at its best and the agility of the bakers with boiling hot sugar is phenomenal. They have even been known to make wedding bouquets. Charming and unmissable.
www.gamlastanspolkagriskokeri.se

Christmas tree, lights, displays, markets
Don't miss what is reputed to be the largest real Christmas tree in the world, on Stockholm's Skeppsbron in Gamla Stan. Standing an

amazing 38 metres tall, decorated with 5,000 lights and a 4 metre star on the top, this is a real sensation. An absolutely gorgeous sight, particularly on a dark afternoon with all the lights twinkling.

Sergels Torg, near Central Station, has a wonderful display of lights too and giant moose consisting of Christmas lights have been known to 'walk' along the side of Berzelli Park at the very top of Strandvägen in Östermalm.

Not far around the corner, at Stockholm's legendary NK department store on Hamngatan, the windows have stunning Christmas displays for children, with different themes each year. These are so beautifully rendered and can see children and adults alike utterly transfixed, stopped only from staying for hours by the bitter cold of the festive air.

Arguably the best place for really warming hot chocolate, large gingerbread hearts and festive cheer is the Gamla Stan Christmas market. You will find a wonderful choice of Christmas food all smelling highly scented and delicious, with many regional delicacies and sometimes Sami people from Sápmi or Lapland (the Sami prefer to refer to Lapland as Sápmi in their own language) in fabulous traditional dress.

If you want to experience a true Sami market you will need to travel way up north to Jokkmokk. The yearly Jokkmokk winter market is one of the oldest in Sweden with traditions dating back to the Middle Ages. The highlight of the market is probably the chance to go on a reindeer sleigh ride.
www.jokkmokksjulmarknad.se

The ABBA Museum
This is just brilliant. An electric experience worthy of frequent repetition. Housed in a very new wooden building on Djurgårdsvägen, it provides a truly interactive experience where your singing attempts in a recording booth and on stage as the fifth member of ABBA are recorded and downloadable using your ticket code. There is a full history of the iconic band, as well as a glittering

array of their costumes and gravity defying boots, not to mention the helicopter they used for world tours. Once again, utterly brilliant – you will come out bouncing and this is the perfect way to while away dark winter afternoons.
www.abbathemuseum.com

Gröna Lund
Another feature of the Djurgården skyline, this theme park is a thrill a minute, right in the middle of Stockholm. Highlights include the Giant Wave Swinger which swings you round a massive pole at an incredible height, a huge freefall tower, a vertical spinning rollercoaster, an 80m Giant Drop and ghost trains. For the smaller, or less intrepid, there is a lovely collection of vintage car rides, 'flying' elephant rides and Pettson and Findus' house. This can be an incredibly busy place, particularly at weekends, so be prepared to get there early or be extremely patient.
www.gronalund.com

The Viking Museum
Recently opened, the Viking Museum on Djurgården offers a first-hand, vivid view of the Viking world with films, sounds effects, archaeological objects and an adventure ride bringing this fascinating age to life through the voyage of Ragnfrid. The ride is not for the faint-hearted and the minimum recommended age is 7. The focus is on an interactive experience and Viking-clad guides are at hand to answer any questions.
www.thevikingmuseum.com

Armémuseum
The Army Museum charts Sweden's history since the 16th century,

focusing on how the Swedish people have been affected by war and conflict. Battle dress, uniforms and weapons are beautifully displayed with everything from the great Nordic War to the Finnish war to the Cold war imaginatively brought to life.
www.armemuseum.se

Skansen
Another of Djurgården's highlights, this is the world's oldest open-air museum, featuring model farms and homesteads from across Sweden, really bringing Sweden's country roots to life. There is also a fantastic zoo focusing on wild Nordic animals such as wolves, moose, lynxes, seals, bears for the sharp-eyed, many birds and Europe's largest herbivore, the bison. You can also warm up in the excellent Baltic Sea Science Centre which houses some fascinating aquariums. There are usually large celebrations for Midsummer at *Skansen* too.
www.skansen.se

Naturhistoriska Riksmuseet
Stockholm's Natural History Museum is a real haven particularly on cold or dark days. It is massive in size and scope, some of the most compelling exhibitions being Swedish Nature, the showcasing of wildlife from the Polar regions and exhibitions centred on human evolution. The Cosmonova is extremely popular, offering IMAX films about nature on its amazing dome-shaped screen – a real wow!
www.nrm.se

The Butterfly House & Ocean Aquarium
Hagaparken is one of the most spacious Royal parks around Stockholm and affords wonderful opportunities for long walks. Near the entrance you will find the *Fjärilshuset*, an enchanting, small butterfly house with more than 700 varieties of mostly exotic butterflies. This is a great pick-me-up on a cold winter's day – do be prepared to carry a lot of your warm clothing if visiting in winter, as the temperature inside never falls below 25 Celsius and the atmosphere is very humid. Right next door is the Ocean Aquarium, particular highlights including shark 'pups' from parents in France and a sample coral reef explaining the dynamics of this fragile

environment.
www.fjarilshuset.se

Sweden International Horse Show
This is a truly superb show of world-class show jumping, dressage and carriage driving, with horses and riders young and older operating at the very highest levels. It is also huge fun, with a Shetland Steeplechase, often hilarious and closely contested dog agility competitions and visiting horses from all over the world. Reflecting Sweden's absolute devotion to horses, it is very well-attended and a great occasion and takes place in the Friends Arena near Solna usually in late November.
www.horseshow.se

Events at Avicii Arena (previously known as *Globen*)
Avicii Arena is one of Stockholm's main arenas and hosts an incredible range of events all year, from ice hockey and football matches, to figure skating championships and Disney on Ice, to pop concerts. The building itself is fascinating, being the largest spherical building in the world, right in the heart of Stockholm. If you want a fantastic view of Stockholm take the Sky-view, a 130 metre (425 feet) lift, right up to the top of the globe.
www.stockholmlive.com

Best parks and rides in Stockholm

One of the prettiest parks in Östermalm is Humlegården. In winter this is where children will try their sledging skills down its tiny hill when the first comes. In Vasastan each winter an ice rink is prepared for skating on the football field. Kungsträdgården park is well worth a visit in spring when the cherry tree blossom arrives - these trees were donated by Japan to King Carl XVI. It is a fleeting, very beautiful moment, so get there quickly as soon as you hear the blossom is out.

The number 7 tram is very popular with children, leaving from T-Centralen past Nybroplan at the top of Strandvägen and is the one sporting a large cream teacup. It operates mostly at weekends during the summer months and serves coffee en route. This is the perfect way to take in the beautiful sights over the water from Strandvägen and travel to the multitude of attractions on Djurgården. Note that you must buy your ticket before getting on!

Djurgården itself is Stockholm's largest park and used to be the royal hunting ground. You can walk and cycle for miles, feeling as if you are in the middle of the country – truly a treat in a capital city and in a really cold winter, you can even skate across to it.

Soft play - Indoor playgrounds *Lekland*

Sweden is blessed with many soft play centres, which can be a godsend on wet autumn days. Perhaps the best-known is Lek o Bus, which offers a huge variety of slides and apparatus to explore and climb on. There are rooms for birthday parties too. There is also Kataach in Tyresö, which has both indoor and outdoor activities.
www.lekobusnacka.se
www.kaatach.se

Kulturhuset

This is a real hub for all forms of culture for children at Sergelstorg with theatre, dance, concerts, art workshops, book readings, circus skills, photography....there's always something on and children can be inspired for hours.
www.kulturhusetstadsteatern.se

Space
In 2021 a new digital culture center was launched in the center of Stockholm (Sergelgatan 2) bringing the largest online communities together under the same roof. They offer an inclusive environment for young and old to connect, collaborate and create. Here you can also find the Avicii Experience – an interactive museum celebrating the memory of Tim Bergling more known as the artist Avicii
www.aviciiexperience.com
www.space.cc

Ocean bus
Sightseeing with a SPLASH! This ride is an experience for both young and old. See Stockholm from both land and water in one single vehicle - an amphibious bus! You will get to see many of the city's best known attractions whilst a guide tells fun and interesting stories along the way. The tour starts on Strömgatan - close to the Royal Opera.
www.oceanbus.se

Outside Stockholm

Tom Tits Experiment

This is an absolute hit for curious children and adults interested in engaging in hands-on science and technology experiments. It is a mere half hour's journey from Stockholm, in Södertälje. From marble runs, to illusions, to acceleration, to magnets and electric circuits, the museum has everything to fascinate budding scientists. There are more than 400 hands-on experiments spread over four floors and throughout a large park that is open spring and summer. Don't miss the very popular soap bubble show!

www.tomtit.se

Kolmården

A fantastic safari park with a huge range of animals both exotic and Scandinavian comprising 1.5 square kilometres of parkland, this is an excellent excursion from Stockholm (170km south) and you can stay the night too. The Safari Camp is probably the most exciting option, allowing you to stay in a tented camp in proximity to the animals. One of the absolute highlights in the park is the Safari Gondola, which allows you to ride above wandering moose, lions, bears and giraffes and get a superb bird's eye view. There are excellent dolphin and bird of prey displays, as well as *Bamses Värld* devoted to the famous large bear and with a great range of rides and attractions.

www.kolmarden.com

Järvzoo

Dedicated to showcasing Scandinavia's wild species, many regard this as being Sweden's best zoo. The focus is on animals living in their own natural environment and you can see everything from Arctic foxes, to lynxes, wolves, moose, musk ox and reindeer, as well as a wonderful variety of owls and other birds of prey at fairly close range. This can be most exciting at feeding time. The whole experience is very attractive in a lovely setting and Järvsö has many other highlights, including a small but very well-designed ski resort, a beautiful river and lots of good spots for foraging for mushrooms in the autumn. Järvzoo Varghotell offers good accommodation in a converted barn and the best view of the wolves, which can also be enjoyed from the sauna.

www.jarvzoo.se

Sports Activities for Children

You may be surprised that most sporting activity for children in Sweden does not take place in school. They will probably have some gym lessons there, but otherwise it is up to you to plan sport after school and this takes place through local clubs and teams.

For football, the best place to start is by looking up the IFK (football club) of your local area on the internet or going to the central sports website www.idrottonline.se. You are likely to find a huge choice of training and match options. Football is taken very seriously in Sweden and this can become quite some commitment but is really inspiring. There are also camps in the Easter and summer holidays. Near Stockholm, clubs in Stocksund, Djursholm, Enebyberg and Täby have excellent reputations, whilst in the city itself, you might like to try Östermalm, Bromma or Sältsjobaden.

Sailing

Sailing is hugely popular and again, you will find many camps available in the holidays. These also offer teenagers masses of opportunity to act as coaches. Great opportunities near Stockholm are at the sailing clubs in Djursholm, Viggbyholm and Sältsjobaden. There are also courses in the summer on Sandhamn in the archipelago. Consult *www.ksss.se.*

Ice Skating/Ice Hockey

Ice skating lessons are a key part of the winter and offered to all ages. DASK in Djursholm is friendly and very active and can also be found via the *www.idrottonline.se* website. You will also find ice hockey available here.

Gymnastics
There is a fantastic gymnastics club in Enebyberg, 20 minutes north of Stockholm, which is one of the 10 largest in Stockholm. It is very vibrant, with 1,400 members and inspires both boys and girls to take part in competitions.
www.enebybergsgymnasterna.se

Also, on Lidingö and Gärdet you have a choice of 70 different gymnastic groups.
www.lidingogymnastikskola.se

Sports Camps etc.
There are also lots of outward-bound holiday courses which are great fun – your local area's (*kommun*) website is a good place to start. The emphasis is on young people taking responsibility, so don't be surprised if a few highly motivated teenagers are in charge of your little person for the week. A fantastic company for this is *www.sportcamp.se* which offers a superb range of opportunities and variety of sports, both in Sweden and abroad.

Other activities for children
Like sport, music lessons mostly take place after school. The best way to find music teachers, music groups, bands and orchestras is to contact the *kulturskola* for the *kommun* where you live. The largest one in the Stockholm region is in the city itself, but just outside, Danderyd's Kulturskola is very active - email *kulturskolan@danderyd.se*. The system is tax-funded which is why you must use the school in your area. For other areas and activities consult: *www.kulturskolan.stockholm.se*

If you want to go privately, entities such as Opus Norden offer singing and instrument lessons, as well as courses and groups.
www.opusnorden.com

How to get around in Stockholm

Taxi

If you choose to take a taxi, we suggest you use either Taxi Stockholm, Cabonline or take an Uber. Taxis in Sweden aren't regulated and if you use other taxi companies you might end up with a very hefty fare. You can compare prices by looking at the yellow sticker they are required to display on their window - this indicates their price based on a 10km / 15 minute journey which should be approximately SEK 300-350.

www.taxistockholm.se   phone: +468150000
www.cabonline.com

Public Transport

The local transport network is called SL and you can use the same ticket on local trains, the tram, the underground/subway as well as SL boats. The easiest way is to either use their app or purchase an ACCESS card. The card can be topped up electronically or at stations, but if you travel frequently you might consider a monthly ticket.

In 2021 SL installed a new system whereby you can purchase one adult fare ticket by tapping your debit card or a digital contactless card such as Samsung Pay, Google Pay, Apple Pay and Fidesmo Pay (in your digital wallets) on SL's electronic readers. The card must be connected to one of the following: Mastercard, Visa or American Express. One ticket per card and it is valid for 75 minutes.

Note that you must have a ticket before getting on board – you can't simply buy a ticket once you've jumped on. Using public transport is by far the best way of getting around and for sightseeing, as parking cars in Stockholm can be time-consuming and quite expensive. The underground/subway with its 100 stations is often referred to as the 'world's longest art gallery' and we can highly recommend one of their free guided tours. The line from Kungsträdgården is a good place to start if you want to take a tour of the underground on your own.

Unfortunately, at the time of writing they do not have a travel planner in English on their website - so you will have to rely on Google translate!

By Boat
A fabulous way of seeing Stockholm is from the sea. You can do this as a tourist and book a tour with Strömma, but why not start off on your own using the great public transport system?

There are four ferry routes included under the umbrella of the SL public transport network and you can use the ACCESS pass as mentioned above. Boats run from the city centre to the Stockholm archipelago, but also to some useful spots between the city's islands and on Lake Mälaren.

Route 82
The Djurgården ferry goes between Slussen (at the southern tip of Gamla Stan) and the island of Djurgården via a jetty on the eastern side of Skeppsholmen (you have to tell them if you want to get off on Skeppsholmen).

Route 80
Then you have the ferry that connects central Nybroplan with Ropsten, stopping at Allmänna Gränd on Djurgården along the way. This route is great if you want a nice trip to the museums on Djurgården or would like an outing to Nacka Strand where you can stop for lunch or a drink by the water at Restaurant J. Another great pit stop en route is for a pizza at 450 Gradi in Dahlénum on the island of Lidingö, or why not enjoy some *fika* while watching the boats in summer at Café Blokhusporten.

If you're living in Djursholm, you can take the commuter boat which forms part of Route 80. It makes a circuit between Ropsten, Tranholmen, Ekudden, Sticklinge brygga, Storholmen, Södra Mor Annas brygga, Storholmen, Östra Frösvik and back. The timetable may vary during the winter owing to ice. People are increasingly using this as a picturesque way of getting to work in Stockholm!

For more details and timetables consult:
www.sl.se

Route 83
This boat will take you even further out into the archipelago, from Strömkajen (by the Grand Hotel) via Slussen and out to Vaxholm. This is a wonderful longer outing - give yourself plenty of time to wander amongst the picturesque pastel-coloured wooden houses around Vaxholm's town centre. You can also visit the 16th-century Vaxholm fortress, built on a little island to defend Stockholm, which now houses a museum chronicling the building's history. Norrhamnen, the harbour, is lined with fishing cottages.

Route 89
This one will take you out to Lake Mälaren (as long as it doesn't ice over!) to the island of Ekerö. It leaves a few times a day but will take you all the way from Klara Mälarstrand (the jetty between the Sheraton and the City Hall) out to Ekerö. In addition, line 89 (Ekerö–Stockholm) shuttles between Tappström and Klara Mälarstrand, via Kungshättan, Ekensberg and Lilla Essingen.

Waxholmsbolaget runs boat and ferry services in the Stockholm archipelago from Arholma island in the north to Landsort on Öja island, in the south.

The services form part of the public transport system in Stockholm County and run all year round, to provide residents, companies and visitors with connections between islands and several mainland

harbours. It is not, however, part of the SL Access ticket system so tickets are purchased either onboard, at the ticket counter or at the self-service machine. Cash is not accepted!
www.waxholmsbolaget.se

Bicycles are permitted on most boats but not in the underground or on trams or buses.

Castles Near Stockholm

In and around Stockholm, you will find a gorgeous choice of castles, many of which are set in beautiful waterside locations often on the banks of Lake Mälaren. Many are open to the public, but be warned that for some the season is very short, so you will need to pack in as many as possible between May and early September. Many have restaurants as well as overnight accommodation and offer reasonable weekend packages.

www.countrysidehotels.se has a great selection of these, as well as other charming, historical places to stay in Sweden. A lovely experience and a perfect way to get a real sense of Swedish architecture and history from the inside.

Skokloster
Set beside Lake Mälaren, Skokloster is one of Europe's finest Baroque castles, built during Sweden's Age of Greatness, between 1654 and 1676, when the country was at the height of its powers. The apartments have fabulous collections of paintings, silver and textiles, as well as beautifully adorned windows and ceilings with typical Swedish flower designs. One of its most famous paintings, Vertumnus by Giuseppe Arcimboldo, is extraordinary but amazingly beautiful - a representation of Holy Roman Emperor Rudolf II as the Roman God of the Seasons, his face rendered in fruit and vegetables. It's also rumoured that Carl Wrangel, the big-spending owner of Skokloster, had a quick temper and would herald dinner by firing one of the mini cannons which form part of his incredibly extensive weapon collection. This is a fabulous spot and also sometimes houses exhibitions of paintings or interiors. It can be reached by boat from Stockholm – consult *www.stromma.se* for timings.

Taxinge Slott
This beautiful castle 60km south of Stockholm on the banks of Lake Mälaren is really brought to life, with reputedly the biggest selection of cakes in Europe on offer in its café, sometimes spilling over into its beautiful Chinese salon. August Strindberg, Sweden's pre-eminent

playwright is said to have been inspired to write his masterpiece 'Miss. Julie' here and it hosts the largest and most sensational Christmas market in Sweden every year. This is a real treat, with an incredible selection of the country's best craftsmen, handicrafts and culinary specialities. The most magical way to arrive is by steam train from nearby Mariefred, an experience which really takes you back in time, particularly as the gas lights are lit on your return trip.
www.taxingeslott.se

Gripsholm
This castle is simply exquisite, its distinctive four domes cutting an elegant silhouette against the waters of Lake Mälaren. It is situated in the sublimely peaceful and enchanting small town of Mariefred, where time seems to have stood still. Enjoy bike rides by the lake side, the wonderful atmosphere of the steam trains and the chance to collapse in a comfortable chair to indulge in the fabulous tea and sticky chocolate cake served at Gripsholms Vardshus which also serves excellent lunches and has gorgeous bedrooms. The castle itself is absolutely fascinating. Having been built by Gustav Vasa in 1537, it features the Swedish State Portrait Collection, incredibly lavish Royal apartments and arguably the absolute highlight – Gustav III's Theatre. This is simply stunning and enveloping – a small scale theatre and Sweden's best preserved from the 18th century, built into one of the castle's domes. It has the feeling of a magical bubble and you can enjoy it without watching the 9 hour long plays to which Gustav's courtiers were sometimes subjected.
www.kungligaslotten.se
www.gripsholms-vardshus.se

Steninge Slott

It is probably the yellow and white façade of this castle which is its most beguiling feature, overlooking Lake Mälaren not far from Sigtuna. The castle was built in 1705 by Tessin the Younger, who also built the Royal Palace in Stockholm. It is privately owned and not open to the public, but you can visit its magnificent stone barn which in winter hosts one of Sweden's very best Christmas markets. Combine your visit with lunch in the excellent restaurant. Well worth a visit.

www.steningeslottsby.se
www.destinationsigtuna.se/en/partner/steninge-castle

Näsby Slott

(1665)

This palace was designed by famous Swedish architect Nicodemus Tessin whose most important works include Drottningholm Palace, as well as Skokloster. In 1897 Näsby Slott was destroyed in a fire rebuilt 1905 following the architect's drawings which had survived the fire.

www.nasbyslott.se

Ulfsunda Slott

(1644)

Here you can have a good meal and stay overnight. Why not try a sauna and a dip in the lake?

www.ulfsundaslott.se

Hesselby Slott

(1650)

A castle focusing on music. If you're looking to relax and enjoy good food in a laid-back setting Hesselby Slott, Sweden's castle of music, is situated in Stockholm and is run by passionate music lovers. One of the owners is popular Swedish singer Tomas Ledin.

www.hesselbyslott.se

Görvälns Slott
(1675)
A colourful and kitsch castle by Lake Mälaren for meetings or just a pleasant weekend. It is adults only (guests over 16 welcome).

Rosersbergs Slott
This palace is a 10-minute drive from Arlanda airport and also includes a museum. Rosersbergs Palace is one of the 10 Royal Palaces of Sweden and the only one you can stay in as a non-royal or visitor. It was built as Karl XIV Johan and Queen Desideria's summer Palace.

The Royal Palace, Stockholm
Completed in 1760 as a quasi-Roman palace, you cannot miss this vast Baroque edifice as you look across the water from the Grand Hotel side of Östermalm. But it's rather forbidding, beast-like exterior belies some exquisite interiors, within which are worthy of several visits. The massive interior staircase within is imposing to say the least, but less so than you might think as what appears to be marble is actually painted. It took many years for the palace to be built, design preferences changed and it became very much the fashion to work with the *trompe l'oeil* technique, creating the optical illusion that depicted objects in three dimensions.

The Royal apartments are exquisite, Gustav III's bedchamber being particularly fascinating as it was modelled to a certain extent on Versailles, allowing for the morning ritual of the King's *levée* dressing ceremony in front of his courtiers. The ballroom is magnificent, with fabulously intricate flooring. King Karl XI's Gallery is sensational - inspired not a little by Versailles' Hall of Mirrors, it is used for the Nobel Prize dinner hosted by the King and Queen. There is a wealth of fabulous artwork, silver and china and if you're touring around with children, do get them to count the number of clocks in the palace. It's a great distraction and the collection is incredible.

In the Hall of State, you can see the fabulous Silver Throne made for Queen Christina's coronation in 1650. A true replica of it has appeared in at least two Hollywood films, one with Greta Garbo in the black and white movie 'Queen Christina' from 1933 (available on Youtube). Years later, a throne was needed in another Hollywood film so the producers dusted off the old throne from the cellar and it was re-used in the Blockbuster 'Batman' starring Jack Nicholson sitting on it. The palace is a real wow, not to be missed.
www.kungligaslotten.se

Drottningholm (UNESCO world heritage site)
Home to Sweden's Royal family since 1981, this is a magnificent palace not far from Stockholm on the banks of Lake Mälaren, best accessed by boat from the quay in front of Stockholm's Stadshus. Inspired by the great Baroque palaces of France, Queen Dowager Hedvig Eleonora commissioned it in 1662, around the time when Versailles was starting to be built. It is a triumph of Baroque decoration, the highlight being Hedvig Eleonora's bedchamber, where the lives and fears of the Queen widowed when just 23 and her husband, King Karl X, are beautifully depicted. Queen Dowager Hedvig Eleonora had great influence during the reigns of both her son (King Karl XI) and grandson (King Karl XII).

In 1744 Queen Lovisa Ulrika was given Drottningholm as a wedding present from the King. Coming from German roots and influenced by the ideals of the French Enlightenment, it is said that she was shocked by Sweden's lack of culture and made it her business to redress the balance. A key part of this was the building of the Drottningholm Palace Theatre in 1766.

If you take a guided tour here, you will be told that she imported a master of theatre from France to train the actors – he was frequently on the verge of despair, chiefly because of the abject cold and attempted escape. Fortunately, the theatre came to fruition and today children can delight in the backstage tour, where you can see the workings of the wooden machinery, whilst adults can indulge in the opera season in the summer. Be warned, the chairs are phenomenally hard, so bring lots of cushions! The theatre also has a gorgeous shop, with mask making activities for children and other lovely things to buy.

Apart from changing some of the palace's heavy and dark Baroque interiors to lighter rococo, Queen Lovisa Ulrika also built a splendid library decorated in white and gold. The bookshelves are made from cedarwood with rich wood carvings.

It is well worth ambling through the regal grounds to the Chinese Pavilion. King Fredrik had it built in Stockholm in secrecy and then transported on Lake Mälaren to Drottningholm in time for the Queen's birthday (the birth of prefab housing)!

On the morning of her birthday, her 7 year old son Crown Prince Gustav (who became Gustav III) presented her with the golden key to the Chinese Pavilion. 16 years later the current more sturdy structure replaced the old wooden pavilion from 1753. Don't miss Confidencen here either – a wonderful folly designed for the Royal family to have their meals privately. Hence there is a fascinating pulley system for serving lunch or dinner which came up through the floor, as the family wanted total privacy and no servants to be present. The café at Drottningholm is excellent too!

Royal Swedish Palaces

Solliden Palace on the island of Öland is the only palace privately owned by the King of Sweden and was built in 1906. They also own a country house in Storlien where they often spend Easter cross country skiing. When the King's uncle died, he inherited a villa in Sainte Maxime on the French Riviera. They also lease Stenhammar Palace from the State. The other Royal Residences owned by the State that are included in the Swedish Royal Court are:

- The Royal Palace (Stockholm)
- Drottningholm Palace (Lovön, outside Stockholm). Private residence of the Royal family.
- Gripsholm Castle (Mariefred)
- Gustav III's Pavilion (Haga Park, Stockholm)
- Rosersberg Palace (Sigtuna)
- Ulriksdal Palace (Stockholm)
- Rosendal Palace (Djurgården, Stockholm)
- Tullgarn Palace (Vagnhärad)
- Strömsholm Palace (Strömsholm)

If you are interested in keeping tabs on the Royal family's schedule you can find their official calendar on the following website: *www.kungligaslotten.se*

More Palaces & Castles

Södermanland County is a county or *län* on the south-east coast of Sweden. In the local dialects it is usually shortened and pronounced as *Sörmland*. For palace enthusiasts, there are more than 400 palaces, castles and manors waiting to be discovered in this county. More information can be obtained from the county website: *www.visitsormland.se.*

They make a good day trip from Stockholm and here are just a few:

- Stjärnholm Manor
- Gripsholms Castle
- Öster Malma Castle
- Tullgarn Palace
- Dufwelholm Manor
- Södertuna Palace
- Taxinge Palace
- Säfstaholm Castle
- Ericsberg Castle
- Julita Manor
- Nyköpingshus

If you are into palaces and manors there are many more scattered around Sweden, mainly in the southern parts of the country. These are the most famous and worth a visit when you are ready to discover the rest of the country:

- Läckö Castle - near Lidköping on Lake Vänern.
- Örebro Castle - rebuilt from a fortress into a Renaissance castle in Örebro.
- Kalmar Castle - started off as a fortress in the 12th century on the east coast of Sweden.
- Häckeberga - a manor house near Malmö on its own island, dating back to the 14th century.

- Svaneholms Slott - out on its own island with its own ghosts.
- Sofiero - worth a visit in spring with its more than 10,000 rhododendron bushes.
- Tjolöholms Slott - a more modern palace dating from 1904, probably one of the latest ones built.
- Vadstena - by Lake Vättern.

Museums

In many museums, entry is free and you can enjoy art, architecture, history and culture from near and far. We have already mentioned some museums in the 'For Children' chapter but many of them are also fascinating for the whole family.

Post Museum
Situated in Gamla Stan in what was, until 1869, Stockholm's only post office, the Post Museum is quite simply entrancing. It displays a fascinating history of the postal service in Sweden showing how postmen have grappled with incredibly difficult climate conditions since the 17th century to deliver the post against all odds, including a range of different post vans up to the present day. Perfect for philatelists, but also of broader interest and a diverting pit stop in Gamla Stan on a winter's afternoon.
www.postmuseum.se

Army Museum
Sweden's best historical museum, with exhibitions on three floors. Walk through Swedish history from 1500 to the present day with fascinating historical objects and realistic scenes. Battle dress, uniforms and weapons are  beautifully displayed with everything from the great Nordic War to the Finnish war to the Cold war imaginatively brought to life. Experience living conditions for soldiers, their families and the general public.
www.armemuseum.se

Museum of Ethnography
Museum of Mediterranean & Near Eastern Antiquities
Museum of Far Eastern Antiquities
These three museums are part of the National Museums of World Culture with different themes spanning the whole world and

thousands of years of human culture from prehistoric times to the modern world today.

www.etnografiskamuseet.se
www.medelhavsmuseet.se
www.ostasiatiskamuseet.se

The Hallwyl Collection
In the heart of Östermalm, step back 100 years in time to enter the world and home of Count and Countess von Hallwyl. This 40 room mansion in the centre of Stockholm depicts the life of the rich during the turn of the century, with fabulous collections of artefacts amassed with no eye for expense. It is a gorgeous cocoon in which to luxuriate on a dark day. Guided tours and entry into some of the rooms are subject to a fee.
hallwylskamuseet.se

The Swedish History Museum - *Historiska*
The Swedish History Museum is one of the biggest museums in Sweden. Here you can see Sweden's greatest gold and silver treasures, incomparable medieval art and unique finds from one of the most violent battles of Swedish history – the Battle of Gotland in 1361. If you have a penchant for the Viking era, a brand-new Viking exhibition will open in 2021.

The new '*Ekonomiska Museet*' (previously known as the Royal Coin Cabinet) will also open here. This museum's collections consist of approximately 650,000 objects, including one of the world's first coins, the first banknotes and heavy tin coins, which are the world's largest coins.
www.historiska.se

The Royal Armoury - *Livrustkammaren*
This is one of our favourite museums in the cellar vaults of Stockholm's Royal Palace in Gamla Stan and well worth a visit. Don't miss the most famous item here - Sofia Magdalena's wedding dress which she wore to marry King Gustav III in 1766. When you see it, you might wonder how she ever got into it, let alone through any doorway! Way down in the cellar vaults you can see the fabulous

coaches which have been used during state ceremonies, weddings and funerals.
www.livrustkammaren.se

Maritime Museum
This museum gives an excellent overview of Sweden's maritime past and present. It has everything from a host of model boats, beautiful paintings and naval uniforms, detonators and full size beautifully restored boats, to entire icebreakers. Visit to get a feel for just how important the water is to Sweden's history and identity.
www.sjohistoriska.se

The *Vasa*
The story of the *Vasa*, the world's best preserved 17th century ship, is the stuff of legend in Stockholm. Its mast, emerging from the roof of the museum built specially to house it, dominates Djurgården's skyline from Östermalm or Gamla Stan. Embodying Sweden's imperial prowess during the Great Power Era of that time, she set off on her maiden voyage in August 1628 laden with 64 cannons but would capsize almost immediately, top heavy as she was and with inadequate ballast having been built into the bottom of the ship to make her float securely.

It is a truly astonishing sight in a museum brilliantly conceived to show each layer of the ship to best advantage and really bringing both the vessel and its doomed history to life. Don't miss the excellent film before you look at the ship itself – the story of how it emerged from 333 years of darkness in 1961 is amazing. You will find yourself returning to the *Vasa* again and again, so magnetic is its pull and tragic its fate.

www.vasamuseet.se

The Royal Stables and Changing of the Guard
The immaculately kept Royal Stables provide a serene scene in mid Östermalm – you step off the street into a timeless world of equine calm. The 20 horses are perfectly trained to take part in processions and *cortèges* for state visits and other Royal occasions. These are extremely happy horses, trained daily in spacious Djurgården and put out to meadows in the summer and a delight to see.
www.kungligaslotten.se/english/royal-palaces-and-sites/the-royal-stables

You can hear them trotting down Strandvägen and towards the Royal Palace to assist with the Changing of the Guard, which alternates between a walking or mounted ceremony.

Here is their general schedule but do check their website before setting out:
www.forsvarsmakten.se

> **Summer:**
> The Changing of the Guard ceremony, including a military marching band and parade, is held every day from 23rd April to 31st August. The column marches from the Army Museum or Cavalry Barracks at 11:45am and 11:35am respectively, and 12:45pm and 12:35pm respectively on Sundays and public holidays.

> **Autumn:**
> From 1st September, the parade is generally held on Wednesdays, Saturdays and Sundays, departing from the Army Museum at 11:45am, and at 12:45pm on Sundays and public holidays, accompanied by a military band. If there is no musical accompaniment, the Royal Guards march from the Obelisk.

Winter:
From 1st November, the parade is generally held on Wednesdays, Saturdays and Sundays, departing from Mynttorget at 12:09pm, 1:00pm on Sundays and public holidays.

If you want to watch it from the Palace courtyard, it is worth arriving a little early to get a good vantage point and the ceremony takes about 20 minutes.

The Modern Museum
Moderna Museet collects, preserves, shares and exhibits modern and contemporary art. It opened in 1958, when modern art from the early 20th century and photography from 1840 onwards was moved from the *Nationalmuseum* into a former navy drill hall on Stockholm's Skeppsholmen.

The current building was completed in 1998, adjoining the old museum premises, and is designed by the Spanish architect Rafael Moneo. Have a walk in their gardens outside the museum and see their outdoor collection, from Picasso sculptures (*Déjeuner sur l'herbe*) to cigarette butts ('Last Cigarette')!
www.modernamuseet.se/stockholm/en/

ArkDes - the museum of architecture and design
Situated on the island of Skeppsholmen, this is where the yearly gingerbread house competition is held. The building is just near the Modern Museum, so you can easily combine the two of them in a day together with the Museum of Far Eastern Antiquities.
www.arkdes.se

Nationalmuseum
We have mentioned this museum before under 'Art Galleries'. Here you will find a collection of paintings, sculptures, drawings and prints from 1500-1900 and applied arts, design and portraits from the early Middle Ages to the present day. They have an excellent app with audio tours in English which you can download on your mobile, called Nationalmuseum Visitor Guide. One visit to this fabulous

newly renovated museum is not enough and a suggestion might be to cover one floor at each visit.
www.nationalmuseum.se

The Medieval Museum - *Medeltidsmuseet*
In 1978, building started for an underground parking lot near Parliament - this came to a halt when they came upon archaeological artefacts, as well as parts of the old fortress wall believed to have surrounded Stockholm years before it was actually called Stockholm (in 1252). The parking lot was downsized and the Medieval Museum was created. This is an excellent museum to give you an idea how life looked like during the medieval era in Gamla Stan (The Old Town).
www.medeltidsmuseet.stockholm.se

The ABBA Museum
Just brilliant - an electric experience worthy of frequent repetition. Housed, since 2013, in the ground floor and cellars of the POP house hotel on Djurgårdsvägen, it provides a truly interactive experience where your singing attempts in a recording booth and on stage as the fifth member of ABBA are recorded and downloadable using your ticket code. There is a full history of the iconic band, as well as a glittering array of their costumes and gravity defying boots, not to mention the helicopter they used for world tours. Keep your wits about you - look out for a red telephone in one of the rooms and if it rings, answer! Every ABBA member has its number and it may just ring when you are there. Anni-Frid Lyngstad initiated this idea and she has promised she will randomly call, as will the other members. You will come out bouncing and this is the perfect way to while away dark winter afternoons with friends or family.
abbathemuseum.com

Gröna Lund - colloquially called *Grönan*
Just next door to the ABBA museum is *Gröna Lund*. Apart from it being an amusement park uniquely situated with a panoramic view over the sea, every year sees great artists performing outdoors and you might just find that your favourite artist is performing this year. Past performers include Louis Armstrong, Jimi Hendrix, Bob Marley, Paul McCartney, David Cassidy, Abba, Lady Gaga, Kiss and

Alice Cooper. The theme park is a thrill a minute, right in the middle of Stockholm. Highlights include the Giant Wave Swinger which swings you round a massive pole at an incredible height, a huge freefall tower, a vertical spinning rollercoaster, an 80m Giant Drop and ghost trains. This can be an incredibly busy place, particularly at weekends, so be prepared to get there early or be extremely patient. *www.gronalund.com*

The Viking Museum
Recently opened, the Viking Museum on Djurgården offers a first-hand, vivid view of the Viking world with films, sounds effects, archaeological objects and an adventure ride bringing this fascinating age to life through the voyage of Ragnfrid. The focus is on an interactive experience and Viking-clad guides are at hand to answer any questions. *www.thevikingmuseum.com*

Skansen
Another of Djurgården's highlights, this is the world's oldest open-air museum, featuring model farms and homesteads from across Sweden, really bringing Sweden's country roots to life. There is also a fantastic zoo focusing on wild Nordic animals such as wolves, moose, lynxes, seals, bears for the sharp-eyed, many birds and Europe's largest herbivore, the bison. You can also warm up in the excellent Baltic Sea Science Centre which houses some fascinating aquariums. There are usually large celebrations for Midsummer at *Skansen* too.

On another note, with some 500 choirs Sweden can boast being the country with the highest number of choirs per capita in the world. As well as enjoying singing together when drinking, there is also the phenomenon of *'Allsång på Skansen'* - a singalong for everyone to enjoy outdoors at *Skansen* and broadcast live on TV. This kicks off the summer season and takes place once a week in the evening - young and old sing along to their hearts' delight, accompanying a well-known Swedish musical artist singing popular Swedish songs. *www.skansen.se*

Naturhistoriska Riksmuseet
Stockholm's Natural History Museum is a real haven particularly on cold or dark days. It is massive in size and scope, some of the most compelling exhibitions being Swedish Nature, the showcasing of wildlife from the Polar regions and exhibitions centred on human evolution. The Cosmonova is extremely popular, offering IMAX films about nature on its amazing dome-shaped screen – a real wow!
www.nrm.se

The Nobel Prize Museum
In the Old Town you will find the Nobel Prize museum on the main square (Stortorget) in a building that used to house the Stockholm Stock Exchange. It was built in 1778 - upstairs is the Stockholm Academy from where they announce the winner of the Nobel Literature Prize every year. Downstairs is the entrance to the Nobel Museum, as well as Bistro Nobel where you can indulge in their speciality Nobel Ice Cream cake - before you leave your seat, turn it up-side-down, as a Nobel laureate has signed his name underneath a chair.

Alfred Nobel (1833-1896) had a clear vision for the prize he created. In his will, he wrote that he wanted to reward those who had "conferred the greatest benefit to humankind". Apart from some of the different inventions that have led to the Nobel Prize, you will get an in-depth background and analysis of some of the freedom fighters, writers and scientists who have all made the

greatest contributions to benefit humankind. Showcased in the museum are the laureates' own contributions with personal artefacts which they have donated.

The Nordic Museum
Housed in one of the most impressive buildings on Djurgården, this is Sweden's largest museum of Nordic cultural history. You may need

to make several buildings as there is so much to see in this vast building. On enternig the hall you are welcomed by the monumental oak statue of Gustav I Vasa, King of Sweden from 1523 to 1560 created by Carl Milles together with his wife Olga. The museum's collections encompass exclusive items to everyday objects connected with Nordic lifestyle from the 16th century to the present day.

The City Hall
This is a monumental building in the centre of Stockholm by Lake Mälaren - with its gilded three crowns at its apex, it is difficult to miss! Apart from the City Hall being the office for the City Council it is also famous for its grand ceremonial halls and unique pieces of art. It is the venue for the annual Nobel Prize banquet which is held in the Blue Hall on 10th December each year. More than 1,200 guests are served a fabulous dinner in the presence of the Royal family and the Nobel laureates with their families. Each year a unique menu is

created by a top Swedish chef and served on the special Nobel dinner service which was created by Rörstrand especially for the 90th anniversary Nobel dinner. The Orrefors glassware is exquisite. This is Sweden's take on the Oscars, with fabulous jewellery and beautiful dresses mixed with the pomp
and circumstance of Royal protocol at its best – the event of the year.

Take a guided tour of this outstanding building together with the author, Jessica Dölling Gripberg, next time you are in town.
www.tostockholm.com

Riddarholmskyrkan
This is perhaps the Swedish take on London's Westminster Abbey and where most of Sweden's Royalty are buried. The tombs of 17 regents and their families are in *Riddarholmskyrkan,* which was originally built in the middle of the 13th century as a Franciscan Monastery. As of 1950 the Royal family use Karlsborg island near the Haga Palace as their burial place. *Riddarholmskyrkan* is only open to the public during the warmer months of the year.

The House of Nobility – *Riddarhuset*
One of the most beautiful buildings in the Old Town, Riddarhuset is both a palace and an organisation for the noble families of Sweden. It was the Parliament for the nobility when Sweden was run by its four major estates – the Nobility, the Clergy, the Burghers and the Peasantry (1668-1865). In 1902 the explorer Sven Hedin was the last person in Sweden to be ennobled by the King – this honour is no longer granted.

Music, Concerts & Theatre

There are many theatres, concert and music halls in Stockholm of which we have only mentioned a few which are more geared towards international and English speaking audiences.

Operahuset (the Opera House)
The old opera house was founded in 1782 by King Gustav III. It was a mirror image of the opposite building which still exists and is now the foreign ministry. King Gustav III was shot at the opera and died some days later. The building you see now was inaugurated in 1898 and is Sweden's national stage for opera and ballet.

It is a wonderfully imposing building around the corner from The Grand Hotel and facing the Royal Palace across the water. Arriving amongst the grand columns of its entrance feels very old-fashioned somehow and the foyer inside is no less glamorous. Stockholm certainly delivers the traditional opera house ambience and it is a wonderful setting for a constantly strong programme, encompassing regular productions of Wagner, the Italian greats of opera as well as more *avant garde* offerings in true Swedish style. The quality of performances is fantastic – the only drawback is of course that the words of the score are translated into Swedish on the surtitles, so it may be time to relax into the music rather than try to decipher – between Italian, German and Swedish – exactly what's being said.

Another absolute highlight of the opera house is the lunchtime concerts offered in the Gold Foyer. Envelop yourself in a cocoon of gold stucco and fabulous chandeliers, as superb soloists play while you enjoy a delectable lunch. It's a winning combination, particularly in winter.

The opera house is very proactive with children, offering productions intended to draw the younger audience, as well as weekend workshops and fascinating backstage tours – the size of operations backstage is awe-inspiring and plundering the costume cupboard is pretty good fun too!

Berwaldhallen
Berwaldhallen, was inaugurated in 1979 and built two thirds underground, blasted in to the granite rock, so it appears smaller than it actually is. It is the home stage for two ensembles: the Swedish Radio Symphony Orchestra and the Swedish Radio Choir, which are both among the best in Europe in their respective fields.

Konserthuset
This is the venue for the yearly Nobel Prize giving ceremony and the stage for the Royal Stockholm Philharmonic Orchestra. Each year they present hundreds of concerts in various genres, as well as activities for children, guided tours, exhibitions and much more.

The blue concert hall at Hötorget is one of Stockholm's recognisable landmarks with Carl Milles' grouping of sculptures, the Orpheus Well, on the stairway leading into the building. Much of the décor in the vestibule was designed by Einar Forseth – the same man behind the unmissable gilded hall in Stockholm's City Hall. More of Carl Milles' work can be seen in the main foyer.

The Royal Dramatic Theatre - *Dramaten*
The state owned Swedish National Theatre built in 1908 has a mandate from the government to perform classical theatre, newly written Swedish and international theatre, and theatre for children and youth. This art noveau-building on Strandvägen houses five stages with the main stage seating up to 770 spectators. There are also a number of Carl Milles statues here. Many famous Swedish actors have started their careers on this stage, including Ingrid Bergman and Greta Garbo.

Drottningholmsteatern
We have mentioned this unique theatre before, when writing about Drottningholm under 'Castles Near Stockholm'. It was built in 1766 at the request of Queen Lovisa Ulrika. There are performances here during the summer months using the original wooden stage machinery which includes wind, thunder and cloud machines, as well as traps and moving waves all operated by hand. 30 stage sets have been preserved, with themes from 18th century repertoires.

Stockholm English Speaking Theatre
SEST wants to reach out to a wide audience of both native English speakers, Swedes and other nationalities for whom English is their second language. The company is based on a team approach where the ensemble, rather than the individual actor, comes first, a desire to explore language and vastly contrasting themes using and mixing different training methods from the actors' respective countries.
www.sestcompany.com

International Theatre Stockholm
ITS was founded in 2014 by Josh Lenn and Katarina Wahlberg. The vision was to build a fun, warm and welcoming theatre and related international community in Stockholm.

ITS strives to put on shows that not only entertain, but also move people. Its improvised comedy shows have brought together and entertained people from over 40 different countries. The 'Lost in Translation' show won prizes including the People's Choice Award for the Best Show at the Swedish Performing Arts Awards of 2017.

Swedish Music

Music is very much part of the Swedish culture. The Swedish fiddle and *nyckelharpa* are the most common Swedish folk instruments. Traditional folk music with dances such as the polka and hambo often accompany celebrations for Midsummer - so head to *Skansen* if you would like to join in with the dancing. The musicians will be wearing their national costumes representing their different counties.

The Sámi *Yoik* is a traditional form of song performed by the Sámi people of Sapmi and you might find it slightly similar to the chanting of the Native American culture.

In Swedish schools, children get their first introduction to music at a young age, firstly by learning to master the recorder – much to the chagrin of many parents! Singing is also included in the curriculum as well as the opportunity to focus on another instrument or to join one of the many municipal music and arts schools.

Singing in choirs is immensely popular, and you can enjoy listening to these performances in many of the churches which reach a high point in December with concerts for Lucia and Christmas.

Johan Helmich Roman (1694-1758) was a Swedish Baroque composer who spent some years studying music in England and returned to Sweden, becoming the Master of the Swedish Royal Orchestra. He has been referred to as 'the father of Swedish music'. His finest work, *Drottningholmsmusiken,* was composed for the wedding of Crown Prince Adolf Frederick of Sweden and Lovisa Ulrika of Prussia and is a delight to listen to.

Carl Michael Bellman (1740-1795) was a central figure in the Swedish song tradition and a songwriter, composer, musician, poet and entertainer in the court of Gustav III. Many of his songs were drinking songs, which are still being sung today, washed down with *snaps*!

Other well-known Swedish composers include Wilhelm Stenhammar (1871-1927), Hugo Alfvén (1872-1960) and Franz Berwald (1796-1868) whose name is well known to Stockholmers because of *Berwaldhallen* (the concert hall). Edvin Kallstenius (1881-1967) should not be omitted, as his repertoire includes the rearranged folk ballad which is now the Swedish National Anthem (lyrics by Richard Dybeck).

Well before these composers were born, animals could enjoy being herded in by *kulning*, an ancient Scandinavian form of herding call. If you look up Jonna Jinton and *kulning* on Youtube, you can listen to this eery but beautiful ancient chant.

Sweden in its more modern guise is synonymous with Pop music. The annual 6-week song competition extravaganza *Melodifestivalen* or *Mello,* broadcast on SVT, is a major event. It is performed in different cities, culminating in the Stockholm finale. Swedes get the chance to vote for the best song to represent Sweden in the Eurovision Song Contest. The show is fun, topping TV viewing figures and dominating local music charts.

In 1974 ABBA won the Eurovision Song Contest with 'Waterloo', having competed in *Melodifestivalen* the previous year, when they came third with 'Ring Ring'. The rest is music history!

Other well-known Swedish artists of recent times include: Roxette, Ace of Base, Europe, Swedish House Mafia, Avicci, Zara Larsson...just to name a few.

Every country has its take on a birthday song, and this is the Swedish version. The gist of the song is that the person celebrating their birthday will hopefully live for 100 years, pushed on a wheelbarrow (the word pushed in Swedish '*skjuta*' is a homonyme and can also mean 'shot').

Ja, må han leva!
Ja, må han leva!
Ja, må han leva uti hundrade år!
Javisst ska han leva!
Javisst ska han leva!
Javisst ska han leva uti hundrade år!

Och när han har levat
Och när han har levat
Och när han har levat uti hundrade år!
Ja, då ska han skjutas
Ja, då ska han skjutas
Ja, då ska han skjutas på en skottkärra fram!

At the end you will join in an ear breaking crescendo of:

HURRA, HURRA, HURRA, HURRA

If you happen to be celebrating in *Skåne* (the south of Sweden) then
you only say it thrice:

HURRA, HURRA, HURRA!

Day trips from Stockholm

Sigtuna

Built in 970, Sigtuna is the oldest town in Sweden and was, until the 13th century, one of the country's key cities. Less than 50 km from Stockholm, it is situated in a gorgeous spot overlooking Lake Mälaren and is famous for its Viking Rune stones – there is a dedicated walk which helps you follow them. *Mariakyrkan* (St. Mary's Church) harking from the 13th century is another key attraction, but many people are happy to wander down its main street (*Stora Gatan*) which has atmosphere aplenty, beautifully painted house facades in different pastel colours and the signature Swedish deep red, as well as cafés (check out the famous *Tant Brun*) where you can indulge in cinnamon buns or sandwiches piled high. There are also some lovely shops to tempt. This is a place to amble – it's very small and charming. Don't expect too much and you will be delighted.

If you are a Viking aficionado, then you will enjoy following the Sigtuna runestone map.

You can also find the coordinates of all the runestones found in Sweden on this website:

www.runkartan.se

Uppsala

Not far from Stockholm, Uppsala is Sweden's most prestigious university city and often referred to as 'the Cambridge of Sweden'. Founded in 1477, it is the oldest university in the Nordic region and Uppsala's academic credentials are further enhanced by it being the workplace of Carl Linnaeus, botanist, zoologist and father of the modern naming system for plants. Visit the garden dedicated to him in the University Botanic Garden or walk one of the 8 trails dedicated to him to soak up your surroundings.

Or you could do this by canoe or stand-up paddle board along the River Fyris. Or run up the ancient 6th century Viking burial mounds and visit the museum to learn more about Viking heritage in the area. Something more sedate would be the Gothic cathedral which is also where King Gustav Vasa is buried. Otherwise, you may recognise the surname of Anders Celsius, the Swedish astonomer who invented the Celsius temperature scale. Born in Uppsala in 1701 and dying 43 years later, he was the first person to make a connection between the phenomenon known as the *aurora borealis*, or the northern lights, and the magnetic field of the Earth.

Trosa

Beautifully positioned on the Sörmland coastline south of Stockholm, Trosa is a real gem. It is very small, but has a gorgeous canal running through it with very pretty waterside houses and the odd teashop. A little train will drive you through the charming houses in summer, whilst in winter you may want to abandon yourself to the comforts of the *Stadshotell* where bedrooms are pretty, the welcome excellent and the restaurant thoroughly inviting with delicious food. A picturesque spot to enjoy Swedish life at a slow pace or indulge in miles of walking along the coast or endless swimming opportunities. Or you can combine a stay here with a trip to nearby Tullgarn castle. *www.trosastadshotell.se*

Mariefred

We have already extolled the virtues of Mariefred as it is the location of magnificent Gripsholm castle, but it really is the most stunning place and could become one of your absolute favourites. Enjoy the gorgeous wooden painted architecture, the views of the castle across the water, the delights of the castle itself, opportunities to walk in the woods, enjoy wild flowers in spring, cycle and boat. Or for those serious rail enthusiasts, take a ride on the enchanting narrow gauge steam railway or potter around the engine sheds chatting to people who could happily spend every waking hour enthusing about steam. Then relax and ponder all your adventures in the comfort of Mariefred's most beguiling hotel – Gripsholms Vardshus. You won't want to leave! *www.gripsholms-vardshus.se*

Overnight Trips & Hikes

Lake Vättern (1 or 2 nights – summertime)

Drive from Stockholm and visit the area around lake Vättern, Sweden's second largest lake.

In the area you can visit the medieval town of Vadstena with the Abbey and Castle.

'*Rökstenen*' near Ödeshög which features Sweden's most famous rune stone from the Viking era, the longest known runic inscription with 760 runic characters carved in stone. Nearby you can visit the Alvastra monastery ruins.

Borenshult locks - east of Motala with five interconnecting locks with a height difference of 15 metres (built 1823-25). This is part of *Götakanal*, the canal which connects the west coast of Sweden with the east coast of Sweden.

Gyllene Uttern in Gränna is a lovely place to stay. Don't forget to stop in Gränna to see the making of the Gränna *Polkagris* (traditional Swedish candy canes). You can also visit the Grenna museum which shows Andrée's fateful hot air balloon expedition to the North Pole in 1897.

Park the car in Gränna and take the ferry over to the beautiful island of Visingsö (this is a full day trip so you might like to stay overnight - more simple accommodation is offered on the island). Keep a look out for the famous Husqvarna automatic lawn mower robots in every garden!

West Coast of Sweden (summertime)

Lysekil is a pretty town and good base for visiting lots of places by ferry, including the idyllic villages of Fiskebäckskil and Grundsund. You can also just chill out on the rocks or go for long walks along the dramatic coastline and swim in the beautiful sea (weather permitting).

For more inspiration, look at *www.vastsverige.com/lysekil*. Good places to stay in Lysekil are the hotels run by Strandflickornas Strandhotell.
www.strandflickorna.se

For a quieter time, you could stay at Gullmarsstrand in the picturesque restored old fishing village of Fiskebäckskil. Fiskebäckskil is where famous painter Carl Wilhelmson got inspiration for many of his paintings. His magnificent big house in a 'national romantic' style stands out and is today classified as a historical monument which impresses many visitors. You can also visit the marina - a safe haven for sailors in a storm. Here you can eat a delicious meal at Brygghuset, their fish soup is excellent.

www.gullmarsstrand.se

There are some fabulous walks along the rocks by the sea and we can recommend spending a day walking from Fiskebäckskil along a well-marked 6 km trail that passes through the village of Stockevik, ending up in the quaint village of Grundsund. Take a break here for lunch and enjoy watching the boats manoeuvring through the tight channel.

Just across the fjord from Fiskebäckskil is Lysekil with its spectacular and overbearing granite church serving as a beacon for sailors. Lysekil can be reached by ferries that leave on a regular basis just next to the hotel. Lysekil is more of a city, but still has the charm of the west coast with fabulous walks along the sea with views out to sea with its stark granite islands.

On your way home from the west coast, you should take the road going via Lake Vänern and stop at Läckö Slott near Lidköping. You can stay the night and even listen to an opera in the castle courtyard. For further information:

www.vastsverige.com (and search for läckö)
www.lackoslott.se

Sörmlandsleden **trail** (1,000 kilometres long)

Sörmlandsleden is one of the longest walking trails in Scandinavia. The main trail is 627 kilometres long. There are access routes from Stockholm and the paths take you through wilderness, areas of cultural tradition and past historical monuments. There is everything from open landscape, wilderness, lakes and beautiful coastline.

The Sörmlandsleden trail is divided into 92 sections that are between 2 and 21 kilometres long. Along the route are circular loops of different lengths, from an hour of walking to a whole day trip. For the adventurous hiker enjoy staying overnight in many beautifully located shelters but bring along all you need to eat and comfortable bedding.
www.sormlandsleden.se

Dalarna (3 days - summertime)

Travelling in Dalarna is a truly Swedish experience. The mountains, the lakes, red cottages, craft traditions with their quaint painted Dala horses and the beautiful traditional national costumes. The word *Dalarna* means 'the dales' (valleys). The largest lake – Siljan - was formed millions of years ago by the impact of a large meteorite.

The drive up north from Stockholm to Falun in Dalarna takes approximately 3 ½ hours. Falun was a major copper-producing centre for centuries and is known for the huge Falun Mine (you might recall that we wrote about the large *Falukorv*-sausage that also originated from here). There is an on-site Mining Museum with interactive exhibits. In town, Dalarnas Museum displays folk art, furnishings and costumes.

We suggest you aim for beautiful *Lilla Hyttnäs*, the home of artists Carl and Karin Larsson in Sundborn, just north-east of the city of Falun. If you are into hiking, then park your car by the Falun ski area called '*Lugnet*'. From here you have a lovely 8.5 km hike (5.3 miles) along the Carl Larsson path through the woods taking you all the way to Carl and Karin Larsson's home *Lilla Hyttnä*' in Sundborn (now a museum). Don't forget that after your visit to *Lilla Hyttnäs*, you will have to walk all the way back to Falun to where your car is parked.

If you prefer, you can drive from Falun to Sundborn which only takes 15 minutes. Having visited Sunborn, drive on to the village of Tällberg (45mins.) where you can stay the night at the renowned old family hotel Åkerblads, dating from the 15th century. Apart from good meals in their restaurant they also have a newly built spa where you can relax after your arduous hike.
www.akerblads.se

Whilst in Dalarna, do visit the Zorn Museum in Mora - the world's largest collection of paintings by artist Anders Zorn (1860-1920). Don't miss a tour of his home next door. Mora is also where thousands of tired skiers cross the finishing line of the world's oldest cross-country ski race, '*Vasaloppet*', a tough 90km (56 mile) race from Sälen to Mora, on the first Sunday in March.

In Mora a special small sheath knife known as *Morakniven* has been in production for more than 400 years. An essential high quality, sharp knife for camping, hiking, fishing or hunting is now produced with a variety of different blades and handles tailored to their specific use.

Nearby in Leksand is the Hildasholm house, (originally known as Stengården), a wedding gift from doctor and writer Axel Munthe to his British wife Hilda Pennington Mellor. The house, built in 1910, is beautifully preserved as are the park and gardens.

Fryksås should be another stop on this tour. Here you can stay overnight at the charming *Fryksås Hotell & Gestgifveri*. Dinners served here are excellent and don't be surprised if you find sticky toffee pudding on the pudding/dessert menu - chef Scotty Ferguson from New Zealand settled here after falling in love with a girl from Dalarna. Apart from this delicious pudding, he serves local ingredients such as bear carpaccio or slow cooked reindeer. From the hotel you have an uninterrupted, magnificent view over Dalarna and lake Orsa with endless hiking and biking trails just next door.

Dalarna (wintertime)

If you want to experience the first (and last) snow of the year and not have to travel too far up north, Dalarna is a safe bet. There are plenty of places to stay but we suggest making the 4 ½ hour journey from Stockholm to Fryksås.

There are endless, well-prepared cross-country tracks as well as Alpine skiing in this area. As we mentioned earlier, the most comfortable option for accommodation would be *Fryksås Hotell & Gestgifveri*, which serves excellent meals. You can either check into one of their rooms or have your own cottage (some have open fireplaces and saunas).

If downhill skiing is more your cup of tea, then the large skiing area of Orsa Grönklitt is just nearby, with plenty of accommodation and slopes just outside your door.
www.orsagronklitt.se

The Jämtland Triangle (3 day hike - summertime)

If you want to be a bit more adventurous and avoid using the car, you can travel by train and discover other parts of Sweden. Experience this 47 kilometre (30 mile) hike set out by STF (*Svenska Turistföreningen* - the Swedish Tourist Association) which includes hostels in Storulvån, Sylarna and Blåhammaren. This takes in the core of the Jämtland Triangle which is one of the most well-known and classic hikes in Sweden.

You can board the night train from Stockholm arriving in the early morning in Duved. From there you take a bus to STF Storulvån where you may want to stop for a meal. Start the first day of your hike and aim for the simple mountain hostel set high in the Sylarnas mountains on the border of Sweden and Norway (*STF Sylarna*). Dinner and overnight stay at STF Sylarna.

On the second day after a hearty breakfast your hike will take you to STF Blåhammaren, the simpler of the hostels. Dinner and overnight there. The final leg of your 3 day hike will be from Blåhammaren to STF Storulvån, where you might have time for a meal before returning to Duved to catch the night train back to Stockholm in the evening. Early arrival the next day by train to Stockholm.

On this hike you can make do with only a lightweight backpack, as breakfast and dinner can be had at the hostels - however, remember to bring along plenty of energy boosts and snacks as well as packed lunches. You can drink water from clear streams along the way. If you have enjoyed Jämtlandstrriangeln then you are ready to experience the rest of Sweden's '*Fjällvärld*' - the mountainous north with its endless hiking trails and fabulous scenery.

Kungsleden & Kebnekaise (summertime)

The Kungleden hiking trail is possibly Sweden's best and one of the most famous in the world. The path is more than 400 kilometres (248 miles) long, passing through four national parks: *Abisko*, *Stora Sjöfallet*, *Sarek* and *Pieljekaise*.

For more adventurous and experienced hikers, the icing on the cake would be Mount Kebnekaise. At 2,106 metres (6,909 feet) it is the tallest mountain in Sweden. The scenery on your way to the summit is stunning. The best time of the year for this ascent is June when there is still some snow on the mountain, which makes both the ascent and the descent easier, as well as there being fewer climbers around. There are two main routes to the summit and we recommend you go with a guide, especially the eastern route.

For more information consult:
www.swedishtouristassociation.com

Unusual Places To Stay

There are plenty of funky places to stay in Sweden, mostly using the great outdoors to optimal effect. These experiences can be wonderful – you're so close to nature, it's refreshing, everything is so unspoilt. It's worth just being armed with a bit of inside knowledge too!

For Swedes, staying in a *stuga* – a simple wooden house probably painted signature reddish brown or pale yellow in the mountains, forest or archipelago – is the quintessential getaway. It certainly is, but it's also fairly 'back to basics', so to enjoy the experience as much as possible it's helpful to know what to expect. It's very likely that your loo will be outside in a small hut - an outhouse or in Swedish, *dass*. There will probably be a notice inside the door extolling the ecological virtues of the loo and saying that it doesn't smell. Whether it does or not is subjective. As you may also need to use it at night, take a little torch as well as loo paper. Secondly, terms of engagement when you rent a house or indeed stay with friends, are very different in Sweden. In both cases, you might be expected to make up the beds yourselves. Whereas you may be used to the delight of ready-made, enticing beds with fluffy pillows, here it's DIY. Similarly, when you leave a *stuga* or rental house, you are entirely responsible for cleaning it and leaving it in the sort of state in which you would like to find it. This should be a virtuous circle and if everyone obeys the rules, then all is well. Just plan time to do this and be sure to adhere to all guidance on litter disposal.

Grinda, Finnhamn & Sandhamn
If you're willing to make these little sacrifices, then the door is open to staying in some amazing spots. The Stockholm archipelago is bursting with enchanting *stugor*, some with their own little fishing boat, others with tiny jetties, all with masses of atmosphere. The best place to find one is *www.airbnb.com* or otherwise many of the larger islands in the archipelago have their own websites, such as Grinda, Finnhamn and Sandhamn.
www.grinda.se
www.finnhamn.se

www.destinationsandhamn.se

Fejan or Island Lodge
Or you could try one of the glamping options available, which bring you really close to nature and the water too. Fejan is a wonderful place in the outer reaches of Stockholm's archipelago (*www.fejanoutoor.se*) or otherwise try Island Lodge in the middle section of the archipelago, where the chef will prepare your dinner and you indulge in a sauna too – it's billed as being the perfect combination of hardship and luxury!
www.islandlodge.se

Tree Hotel
If distance isn't an issue, there is a Tree Hotel at Harrads, some 11 hours' drive north of Stockholm, where options include a UFO up a tree, a mirror cube and a bird's nest. This is truly pushing boundaries and a great place to see the Northern Lights from September to March!
www.treehotel.se.

Utter Inn or Jumbo Jet
You can spend the night under water at Utter Inn, a hotel floating on Lake Mälaren near Västerås, 80 kms north of Stockholm and wake up surrounded by fish looking in at you (*www.visitvasteras.se*). Or sleep in a jumbo jet (the cockpit room comes at a premium) just near Arlanda airport (*www.jumbostay.com*).

Ice Hotel
Perhaps the best known extreme accommodation option in Sweden is Jukasjärvi's ice hotel, near Kiruna. First opened in 1989, it is obviously rebuilt every year and open from December to April. Be warned that the Ice Hotel Winter is what it says on the ticket and your bed will be made of ice, with skins on it for insulation. So, you need your very warmest clothes and sleeping bags, and if you're allergic to animal hair, opt for the actual indoor hotel rooms instead. 12 ice suites are created bespoke by international artists. This place is a wonder, with prices to match but it's not an experience you will forget. Just make sure you choose the option that best suits your

stamina!
www.icehotel.com

Igloo
Or if you really want to have a story to tell, go up to Åre in the north and spend the night in an igloo. Prepare with a delicious warm dinner, followed by a hot spa before sleeping in your igloo. The only creature comfort is a rather beguiling wooden front door. Dress code: Arctic!
www.iglooare.com

Arctic Gourmet Cabin or Nyrup
Way up north, the most recent unusual overnight stay, awarded the Travel Hospitality Award and boasting the world's 'smallest' restaurant, is the Arctic Gourmet Cabin - minimalist but luxurious with your own private chef and sommelier. Travel south to Nyrup and challenge yourself with 'back to nature' living - no running water and the experience of preparing your dinner over an open fire and then retiring to bed in comfortable huts.
www.arcticgourmetcabin.com
www.naturhotell.se

Public Holidays

Apart from the mandatory 25 full days of vacation every year (regardless of your age or type of employment), Swedes have a lot of other holidays. Some are full public holidays - also called *röda dagar* (red days) - but sometimes you are also given half days off before the actual holiday, these are referred to as *klämdagar* (squeeze days).

- New Year's Day
- Epiphany (6th January)
- Good Friday
- Easter Sunday
- Easter Monday
- May Day (Labour Day – 1st May)
- Ascension Day
- National Day (6th June)
- Midsummer Day
- All Saints' Day
- Christmas Day (25th December)
- Boxing Day (26th December)

Midsummer's Eve, Christmas Eve and New Year's Eve are not considered public holidays, but a number of people will be off work.

A Selection of Swedish Recipes

Apart from not being able to find all the ingredients you are used to from home, you may also notice that things you cook just don't taste quite the same.

The very dry climate in Sweden will affect your baking and the recipes provided here work for Sweden. When baking in a very humid country, your dry baking ingredients will attract moisture from the air so you might want to reduce the amount of liquid used in these recipes. My first attempt at Swedish cinnamon buns in Holland was disastrous!

Conversion tables
If using Swedish recipes, you may find the conversions below useful. The main measures in Swedish recipes are krm (*kryddmått*), tsk (*tesked*), msk (*matsked*), and dl (decilitre).

- 1 g = 1 gram = 1/1,000 of a kg
- 1 kg = 1 kilogram = 2.2 pounds (lb)
- 1 dl = 1 decilitre = 100 millilitres (ml) = 1/10 of a litre = 1/2 cup (20 tsk)
- 1 litre = 10 dl = 1.06 quart (qt)
- 1 oz = 1 ounce = 1/32 of a quart (qt) = 28 ml
- 1 lb = 16 oz = 450 ml
- 1 krm = a pinch = 1 ml
- 1 tsk = 1 tsp = 1 teaspoon = 0.17 oz = 5 ml
- 1 msk = 1 tbs = 1 tablespoon = 3 teaspoons = 1/2 oz = 15 ml
- 100°C = degrees Celsius (or Centigrade) = 212°F (degrees Fahrenheit)

If you are at all unsure, you can always buy a set of measuring cups at IKEA or your local supermarket.

Self-raising flour

Add 2 teaspoons of baking powder to each 150g/6oz/1 cup of plain flour.

Sift the flour and baking powder together into a bowl (make sure the baking powder is thoroughly distributed). If you are baking with cocoa, yogurt or buttermilk then also add 1/4 teaspoon bicarbonate of soda (baking soda) as generally these ingredients need a little extra leavening boost.

In the US self-raising flour also contains added salt - around 1/2 teaspoon per cup.

Köttbullar – Swedish Meatballs

Every family has its own favourite recipe for meatballs and the allspice in this recipe can be left out.

For 4 people

> 500 g (18 oz) minced beef and pork
> 1 ½ teaspoon salt
> 1 ½ dl milk
> 1 dl breadcrumbs
> 1 egg
> 1 small yellow onion
> ground allspice (1½ krm)
> pepper (1½ krm)

Soak the breadcrumbs in the milk. Finely dice the onion and slowly sauté in a little butter without browning. Blend the ground meat, diced onion, egg, milk and breadcrumb mixture and the spices - preferably in a food processor or by hand. Add a little water if the mixture feels too firm.

Then shape the meatballs by rolling them in wet hands. Test-fry one meatball to check the taste. Brown a generous pat of butter in a frying pan, and when it 'goes quiet' place the meatballs in the pan and let them brown on all sides (not all at once). Shake the frying pan often. Serve with boiled potatoes and lingonberries.

Gravad Lax – **Cured Salmon**
Take a good piece of salmon, remove any bones and freeze.

> Ikg defrosted salmon
> 1 dl salt
> 1 dl sugar
> 2 tbsp white pepper (crushed in a pestle and mortar)
> Dill (plenty)
> Lemon zest from one lemon

2-3 days before you wish to eat the *gravad lax*, take it out of the freezer and defrost. Mix together the salt, sugar and crushed pepper. Cover the fish with the mixture and lots of dill and lemon zest- place it in a plastic bag. Put the plastic bag in a dish and refrigerate with a weight on top of it. Leave it to cure for 48 hours, turning it occasionally.

When ready to serve, wipe the salmon clean with kitchen paper (removing all the dill and pepper) and cut it in thin slices towards the tail of the fish – preferably with a salmon knife. Serve with *Gravlax* sauce (see recipe), boiled potatoes, dill and lemon.

Gravlaxsås
2 tbsp sweet Swedish mustard (s*enap*)
2 tbsp Dijon mustard
2 tbsp sugar
1 ½ tbsp white vinegar
1 ½ dl oil
2 tbsp chopped dill
salt & pepper (to taste)

Mix the mustard, sugar and vinegar together in a bowl with an electric whisk. Add the oil very slowly whilst whisking. Season with dill, salt and pepper. Ready!

Waffle Batter
For 4 people

125 g butter (*smör*)
2 dl milk (*mjölk*)
4 dl flour (*mjöl*)
2 eggs (*ägg*)
1 tsp sugar (*socker*)
1 tsp baking powder (*bakpulver*)
2 dl cold water a pinch of salt

Melt the butter and let it cool. Whisk together the milk, flour, eggs, sugar and baking powder into a smooth batter. Add the melted butter, a pinch of salt and cold water. Preheat the waffle iron and brush the surface with some oil/butter, so the waffles don't stick. Bake your waffles and when they are ready, place them on a cooling rack so they don't get soggy. Serve them as soon as possible together with a dollop of slightly sweetened whipped cream, some lingonberry or other jam and a dusting of icing sugar.

Kanelbullar - Cinammon Buns

Dough
1 tbsp ground cardamon (*kardemumma*)
2 dl milk (*mjölk*)
1 dl cream (*grädde*)
50 g fresh yeast (*jäst* - red packet)
1 1/2 dl sugar (*socker*)
1/2 tsp salt
100 g butter (salted)
1 egg
approx. 11 dl flour

Crumble the yeast in a large bowl. Melt the butter and then add the milk, cream, cardamon, sugar and salt. Slowly pour the warm mixture (must not exceed 37°c) over the yeast, making sure the yeast dissolves. Mix in the egg.

Add half of the flour, mixing continuously - add nearly all the rest of the flour (leaving 0,5 – 1dl for later) whilst vigorously kneading the dough for about 10 minutes with a large spoon (or in a mixer for 5 minutes). When the dough no longer sticks to the side of the bowl, it is ready. Cover it with a towel and leave it to rise in a warm and draft free area for 45-60 minutes.

Put the oven on at 200°c. Knead the dough on a flat surface with some of the remaining flour. Divide the dough in to 3 pieces. With a rolling pin, roll out each piece of the dough separately into a rectangle (30x25cm).

Filling
200 g soft butter (salted)
1 dl sugar
1-2 tbsp cinnamon (*kanel*)
1-2 dl raisins (*russin*) – this is optional

Spread some soft butter evenly over the rectangle, add the raisins and sprinkle over the sugar and cinnamon. The above filling should be enough for all the dough.

From the bottom up, roll together the rectangle. With a sharp knife cut the roll into 10 equal slices and place each slice into a paper cupcake wrapper or straight on to a tray covered with baking paper. Cover with a towel and allow to rise for about 45-60 minutes.

Sugar & Egg wash
1 dl pearl sugar (*pärlsocker*) or ordinary sugar
1 egg

When ready for the oven, brush the cinnamon rolls with egg wash and sprinkle with pearl or ordinary sugar. Place in the middle of a preheated oven and bake for 7-10 minutes, or until done.

Semlor
(makes 18 large or 30 small)

Buns
2 tsp ground cardamom (*kardemumma*)
3 dl milk (*mjölk*)
50g fresh yeast (*jäst*)
1 1/2 dl sugar (*socker*)
1/2 tsp salt
150g soft butter (*smör*)
1 egg
11-12 dl flour (*mjöl*)

Melt the butter, add the milk and heat to 37° Celsius.

Crumble the yeast into a bowl and let it dissolve with the milk mixture adding the sugar, cardamom, salt and egg.

Add flour (a little at a time) and work into a smooth dough. Let it rise to double the size under a towel for about 40-50 minutes. When ready, turn the dough out onto a floured table. Divide the dough into 18 pieces and roll them into round balls (I prefer small ones so approx. 30). Place them on baking paper on a baking tray and leave to rise under a tea towel for 45-60 minutes.

Set the oven to 200° Celsius.

When they have risen, brush with whipped egg and bake in the oven for 6-7 minutes.

Home made Almond Paste
250 g almonds (*mandel*)
A touch of ground cardamon
Icing sugar to taste (*florsocker*)
Cream

Blanch and peel the almonds, then mix them into a fine powder in a blender. Add sugar, cardamom and mix until it becomes a smooth paste – add a bit of cream to make it smoother.

Once the buns have cooled. Cut out a triangular 'hat' and fill the hole with some of your home-made almond paste. Add some sweetened whipped cream on top of the filling, replace the 'hat', dust with confectioner's sugar and serve (with or without hot milk on the side).

N.B. *semla* is singular, *semlor* is plural

Recycling in Sweden

This is a very complicated, but efficient business in Sweden, so it's as well to know how to navigate it! Swedes have been happy to do their collective duty in recycling for many years and have far exceeded the recycling target for most recyclable waste. For example, the target of 70% for recycled glass by 2020 was already 93% by 2018. There are no landfills in Stockholm so household residual waste is burned in large incineration facilities and this energy is used to produce electricity and district heating.

There are either waste recycling points/stations or shared waste recycling rooms in most rental apartment buildings where you sort your waste. This means that you dispose of your rubbish in different containers. You will be provided with special bags for food waste/organic waste. For more information go to: *www.ftiab.se*

Recycling points/stations -
Sopstation/Återvinningsstation
If you don't have a waste disposal room in your apartment building or if you live in a house, you will most probably find a recycling station nearby. Some municipalities (*kommuner*) may have slightly different ways of handling their waste disposal, so it might be an idea to find out from somebody local.

At the recycling station you can dispose of the following:

- newspapers and magazines
- cardboard packaging
- plastic packaging
- metal packaging
- clear glass packaging
- coloured glass packaging
- batteries

Newspapers and magazines

No envelopes!

Cardboard packaging
Cardboard packaging such as empty cartons can be recycled and used to make new packaging.

Plastic packaging
Both soft and hard plastic can be recycled. You can dispose of items such as plastic packaging and polystyrene foam in the container for plastic. Plastic items that are not packaging, such as washing up brushes and toys, are considered normal waste and are not disposed of here.

Metal packaging
You cannot dispose of metal packaging containing paint or glue or tealight holders in the container for metal – this is hazardous waste, as are aerosol cans, and must be disposed of at a hazardous waste collection point.

Glass packaging
You must separate coloured and clear glass when you are sorting your rubbish.

Food/Organic waste
As mentioned before in most *kommuner* food waste is collected separately in small brown bags and disposed of in separate containers (not by the recycling stations). Food waste may contain:

- remains of fish and shellfish
- remains of meat
- eggshells
- vegetables and fruit
- bread
- tea, coffee and coffee filters
- kitchen paper
- flowers and plants and soil

50% of food waste is turned into biogas energy, so next time you catch the bus it may be running on your waste!

Recycling Centres - *Återvinningscentral*
At these larger recycling centres, you can dispose of bulky waste and larger items such as furniture as well as hazardous waste such as chemicals, paints, solvents and electronic items.

- Electrical Products
- Bulky waste
- Hazardous waste

Electrical products
Electrical waste is the name given to all the electrical items we dispose of. All electrical waste must be disposed of at a recycling centre. This includes light bulbs, fluorescent tubes and everything with an electrical cord or batteries.Batteries must be removed and sorted separately.

Bulky waste
Bulky waste includes old furniture and broken bicycles. If you live in a rental apartment building, you might get help to deal with bulky waste from the property owner. Otherwise, it should be disposed of at a recycling centre.

Hazardous waste
Hazardous waste includes items that may be toxic, explosive, flammable or corrosive and can be harmful in small amounts. Make sure you don't dispose of hazardous waste with normal waste. This is disposed of at the recycling station.

Here are some examples of hazardous waste: car batteries, fuel and oil, paint and glue, chlorine, fluorescent tubes, light bulbs and low-energy light bulbs, solvents, white spirit, paint thinner, turpentine, paraffin and acetone, lighter fluid, rechargeable batteries degreasers and cleaning products.

Normal Household/Residual waste (non-recyclable)

Waste that cannot be recycled is disposed of in the normal container in the waste disposal room (if you live in an apartment) or in the private rubbish bin by your house. You will notice that there is a rubbish bin under the sink in nearly every Swedish home.

What can we pour down the drain?

The only thing you can flush down the loo is loo paper. Other types of paper such as kitchen paper, wet wipes and paper tissues can block the drain and create problems at the sewage works.

Cooking oil should not be poured down the drain and should go with residual waste.

Pant

Each year Swedes recycle nearly 2 million plastic bottles and aluminium cans with a system called *pant*. You return the empty bottle or aluminium can to the supermarket and get your money back. You may have noticed that when you buy your bottle or can that it states the price + *pant*. The *pant* will then be reimbursed once you return the empty bottles.

Bra Miljöval

You can always choose environmentally friendly products marked with the symbols *bra miljöval* or *svanen*.

Medicines

Medical products must be handed in to a pharmacy (*apoteket*). Pharmacies also have special bags for disposing of medicines and special containers for syringes.

Guided Tours

Would you like a bespoke tour just for you, your family or your company?

With personal experience in moving to a new country as an expat and many years as a certified Stockholm guide, Jessica would love to show you Stockholm and give you an insight into 'the Swedish way of life'.

Feel free to contact her and book your own private tour or perhaps a presentation for your foreign employees about 'A Year in Sweden'.

To see what is happening in Stockholm you can follow ToStockholm on:

2Stockholm on instagram

Välkommen!

Jessica Dölling Gripberg
www.tostockholm.com

Useful Contacts & Websites

Grow Internationals
Grow Internationals is an organisation supporting expats and their families who have moved to Sweden. Grow's support focuses on making sure the entire family can settle into their new home and adjust to life in Sweden, by organising Swedish courses, inter-cultural workshops and job coaching services in English. Their community is made up of expats from across the world and there are weekly social events organised in Stockholm and Gothenburg where you can make new friends and contacts. Grow offers membership for the entire family, or individual services tailored to your specific needs.
www.growinternationals.com

New in Sweden (New in Danderyd)
A fantastically useful website which sets out to provide newcomers to Sweden with a wealth of practical information to get you started. It also has particularly detailed information about life in and around Danderyd and all the facilities at hand.
www.newinsweden.com

Newbie Guide
Another very valuable website and a fount of practical information. It also has excellent blogs which give you a really personal insight into many aspects of living in Sweden and adventures to be had.
www.thenewbieguide.se

Undutchables
The focus of this website is giving the international community insights into working in Sweden, as well as publishing job opportunities and offering information about employment. It also has blogs about different aspects of living and working in Sweden.
www.undutchables.se

Thats up
A useful website focused on providing recommendations for

restaurants, bars, clubs and cafes in Sweden's major cities, with a huge depth of information about Stockholm.
www.thatsup.se

Your Living City
This website covers the waterfront of life and what's on in Stockholm, with everything from food, culture, events, music and fitness to practical information about moving to Sweden and setting yourself up in Stockholm.
www.yourlivingcity.com

Visit Sweden
This is Sweden's official website for travel and tourism information and has a wealth of information about all of Sweden's different regions and how best to explore them.
www.visitsweden.com

Visit Stockholm
This website is focused on Stockholm, as the name suggests, with plenty of information about what to do, where to go, what makes the city tick, all brought to life through plenty of vibrant articles providing a stream of ideas of how to enjoy the city your way.
www.visitstockholm.com

ToStockholm
Last but not least, Jessica Dölling Gripberg's own company website which has a wealth of information, suggestions, recipes and links to other useful websites.
www.tostockholm.com

Emergency & Helplines

Government Information
During the Covid outbreak it has been all the more important to keep up with Sweden's policies. To keep up to date with Government announcements consult their website.
www.government.se

Hesa Fredrik – Hoarse Fredrik
Who is he? Well, it is not really a 'he' but the sound that you will hear from warning sirens that are tested all over Sweden four times a year - a hangover of air raid sirens from the Second World War.

The sound test is at 3p.m. on the first Monday of March, June, September and December, with the exception of public holidays. So don't be alarmed if you hear the air raid signal.

The name *'Hesa Fredrik'* was coined by a columnist, Oscar Fredrik Rydqvist at Dagens Nyheter, who in 1930 thought it sounded like him when he had a cold.

If you hear this sound when it isn't being tested, you should:

- Go indoors
- Close your doors, windows and vents
- Turn on Swedish Radio P4 for more information

'If Crisis or War Comes' Brochure
The brochure 'If Crisis or War Comes' describes how those of us who live in Sweden can become better prepared for the consequences of serious accidents, extreme weather, IT attacks or military conflicts.

You can download the brochure in 17 languages from the website or listen to it.

To download the English version:
www.dinsakerhet.se/crisis-brochure

226

Crisis Information
For crisis information and related public announcements go to the website *www.krisinformation.se* and click English on the menu.

112 - SOS
This is the phone number for immediate assistance from the police, fire and rescue services or ambulance. This number can be used as the emergency number throughout Europe. When you call 112, you are redirected to the nearest emergency centre.
www.112.se

113 13 – Information number (in case of accidents and crises)
Call 113 13 for information about major accidents and crises in Sweden. If calling from abroad or from foreign mobile phones in Sweden, call +46 77 33 113 13.

114 14 – Police (not urgent)
Call this number for all non-emergency police matters. If you are calling from abroad or from a foreign mobile in Sweden, call+46 77 114 14 00.

1177 – Medical Advice (not urgent)
This is the phone number for medical advice. You can find more information about this in the chapter about Health

116 111 - Child Helpline
This number has been assigned to BRIS (Children's Rights in Society).
www.bris.se

116 123 - Emotional Support Helpline
This is the phone number for the emotional support helpline. The number has been assigned to the Church of Sweden.

90101 Suicide Prevention - *Självmordslinjen*
The suicide prevention hotline provides a telephone service open 6 a.m. to 12 p.m. which is toll-free. Dial 90101

You can also call in English: tel. 1177, dial 5
Telephone service in Finnish, tel. 1177, dial 8, open 8a.m. to 12 p.m.
Telephone service in Arabic 0771-1177 90, open 8a.m. to 12 p.m.
Telephone service in Somali 0771-1177 91, open 8a.m. to 12 p.m.

Sweden's National Women's Helpline - *Kvinnofridslinjen*
Kvinnofridslinjen offers support to women subjected to violence and threats. Dial 020-50 50 50 or go to their website:
www.kvinnofridslinjen.se/en/

The National Association of Swedish Crisis Centres for Men
Sweden's crisis centres for men offering help with crises and violence.
www.rikskriscentrum.se click on the English link.

Feedback / Contact Us

We very much hope that this guide will become an invaluable companion to you as you discover more and more of what Stockholm and Sweden have to offer and find special places to make you feel at home.

If you have any suggestions as to how we could improve or other information which would be useful, please do not hesitate to get in touch. Equally, we would be delighted to discuss any initiatives for yourself or your company in terms of using the book to deepen understanding of people visiting or coming to live in Sweden and helping them make the most of the experience.

Do contact us by email on:

Stockholmatyourfingertips@gmail.com

With our very best wishes

Alison and Jessica

Disclaimer

All information provided in the guide is accurate to the best of our knowledge at the time of publishing. Owing to the Covid situation, some places are not currently functioning or open in the same way as in normal circumstances and we do not have visibility as to how places will revert as and when the virus situation is alleviated.

Personal Notes

Printed in Great Britain
by Amazon

76840255R00142